dream on

dream on

Bristol writers on cinema

First published in 1994 by New Words, Bristol

ISBN 1 872971 68 7

New Words is a partnership between South West Arts, Redcliffe Press, Avon Library Service and the Bristol / Avon Literature Development Worker, Geraldine Edwards.

'Dream on' has been published with the help and encouragement of the Bristol Cultural Development Partnership.

British Cataloguing-in-Publication Data.
A catalogue record for this book is available from the British Library.

Design and typesetting by 

(01372) 722275

Printed by Longdunn Press Ltd, Bristol

Contents

Foreword

'Dream on' is the second of the New Words books which we hope will encourage local people to write and give an opportunity to all those already filling their own pages to appear in print.

'Dream on' is a book about the universal pastime of going to the pictures. It tells the stories of Bristolians who went to the 'Saturday morning rush', creating mayhem with monkey nuts and orange peel battles, of those who stubbornly sat in their seats to gaze at the big screen while bombs dropped all around them in the1940s blitz, and it tells the stories of romance, love and marriage which all started in the back row.

Hundreds wrote and told us their memories of at least twice weekly trips to the cinema from before the 'talkies' began up until the early 1970s, when many older people just gave up going, feeling that all the romance, dazzle, glamour and pure escapism had left the films. But as early as the 1950s many of the local Bristol cinemas, as familiar to everyone as the local pub, were closing down - many now bingo halls or car salesrooms - because of falling audiences who preferred to watch the box in the living room. Their ' Dream on' memories are crystal clear and razor sharp, they are funny, moving, sad and sometimes just plain nostalgic about the newsreel boys, the cinema cat, brass button inspection time for cinema staff and the smell of disinfectant!

But it's not just about a bygone age. Miraculously, cinemas are now filling up again with young fans of the 'silver screen' and some of course, never went away. Our book contains prose and poetry from present day film-goers with a homage to a local cinema manager, a plea for the British film and a look at what the future might hold.

'Dream on' brings out local people's great affection for the cinema, and along with our first New Words publication, 'Suspended Sentences', it reflects just how many people are writing as a vital creative outlet.

Geraldine Edwards
Literature Development Worker for Bristol and Avon.

Acknowledgements

The publishers wish to thank the many people and organisations who have helped to produce this book, whether with advice, written contributions or illustrations, and in particular: Wally Ball, Bristol Evening Post, Denys Chamberlain, Andrew Kelly and John Winstone. They also thank Faber and Faber for permission to quote from the works of Siegfried Sassoon; and Sinclair-Stevenson, from the works of Cecil Day Lewis. Charles Anderson's *ACity and Its Cinemas* has been a valuable reference source.

INTRODUCTION

The Picture Dancing on the Screen

Andrew Kelly

The literature of cinema is huge though little has been published about the cinemagoer. For the most popular of the arts this is a great loss. The little evidence we have shows how much is missing: we shall never know the full impact of silent film; the importance of cinema to those who went in the heyday of the dream palaces; the wartime years when the movies provided comfort, entertainment and propaganda and - if we do not start recording soon - the impact on the contemporary audience.

Fiction, suitably, has been more imaginative, though few books have covered the audience. Most 'film' novels are about Hollywood and less than ten of these are worth reading. Poetry has been a better companion. Siegfried Sassoon called the cinema 'the picture dancing on a screen':

> And still they come and go: and this is all I know -
> That from the gloom I watch an endless picture-show,
> Where wild or listless faces flicker on their way,
> With glad or grievous hearts I'll never understand
> Because Time spins so fast, and they've no time to stay
> Beyond the moment's gesture of a lifted hand.
>
> And still, between the shadow and the blinding flame,
> The brave despair of men flings onward, ever the same
> As in those doom-lit years that wait them, and have been ...
> And life is just the picture dancing on a screen.

This second book published by New Words is a celebration of cinema by the audience. It attempts to capture the vibrancy, love, frustration, affection of the Bristol cinemagoer in fiction and fact, poetry and prose. The subjects are varied: the Saturday morning rush, usherettes, the back row (a formative influence for many), smoking, the cinema during the dark days of war. One contribution tells of the attempt to resurrect the memory of the Bristolian pioneer of cinematography, William Friese-Greene. Each is marked by a nostalgia for a time enjoyed, a life well spent and - for many - a world now lost.

We go to the movies for many, often contradictory, reasons. The novelist Elizabeth Bowen was asked in 1938 why she went to the cinema. She said:

> I go to be distracted (or 'taken out of myself'); I go when I don't want to think; I go when I do want to think and need stimulus; I go to see pretty people; I go when I want to see life ginned up, charged with unlikely energy; I go to laugh; I go to be harrowed; I go when a day has been such a mess of detail that I am glad to see even the most arbitrary, the most preposterous, pattern emerge; I go because I like bright light, abrupt shadow, speed; I go to see America, France, Russia; I go because I like wisecracks and slick behaviour; I go because the screen is an oblong opening into the world of fantasy for me; I go because I like sitting in a packed crowd in the dark, among hundreds riveted on the same thing; I go to have my most general feelings played on.

Above all cinema is about fantasy. Raymond Durgnat said: 'One's favourite films are one's unlived lives, one's hopes, fears, libido. They

constitute a magic mirror, their shadowy forms
are woven from one's shadowy selves, one's
limbo loves.' Orson Welles said cinema '...has
no boundary...it is a ribbon of dream.'

Fantasy and escapism were best described by
Cecil Day Lewis in 'Newsreel':

Enter the dream-house, brothers and sisters, leaving
Your debts asleep, your history at the door:
This is the home for heroes, and this loving
Darkness a fur you can afford.

Fish in their tank electrically heated
Nose without envy the glass wall: for them
Clerk, spy, nurse, killer, prince, the great and the defeated,
Move in a mute day-dream.

Bathed in this common source, you gape incurious
At what your active hours have willed -
Sleep-walking on that silver wall, the furious
Sick shapes and pregnant fancies of your world.

There is the mayor opening the oyster season:
A society wedding: the autumn hats look swell:
An old crocks' race, and a politician
In fishing-waders to prove that all is well.

Oh, look at the warplanes! Screaming hysteric treble
In the long power-dive, like gannets they fall steep.
But what are they to trouble -
These silver shadows to trouble your watery, womb-deep sleep?

See the big guns, rising, groping, erected
To plant death in your world's soft womb.
Fire-bud, smoke-blossom, iron seed projected -
Are these exotics? They will grow nearer home:

Grow nearer home - and out of the dream-house stumbling
One night into a strangling air and the flung
Rags of children and thunder of stone niagaras tumbling,
You'll know you slept too long.

I fell in love with the moving image from an
early age and it's a love affair that has grown
stronger over the years. I was lucky recently
(though not in my present job!) to be able

regularly to abandon work and visit my local multiplex. I always saw two films, often on my own (which I prefer). The temptation to stay for a third was ever-present but I felt I really ought to leave the darkness and return to work. I was like Walker Percy's moviegoer:

> The fact is I am quite happy in a movie, even a bad movie. Other people, so I have read, treasure memorable moments in their lives: the time one climbed the Parthenon at sunrise, the summer night one met a lonely girl in Central Park and achieved with her a sweet and natural relationship, as they say in books. I too once met a girl in Central Park, but it is not much to remember. What I remember is the time John Wayne killed three men with a carbine as he was falling to the dusty street in **Stagecoach** and the time the kitten found Orson Welles in the doorway in **The Third Man**.

I remember these, just as I remember Jean Simmons singing 'Let Him Go, Let Him Tarry' in **The Way to the Stars**, Humphrey Bogart allowing the Marseillaise to be sung in his café in **Casablanca**, Ginger Rogers doing the 'Black Bottom' with the other prisoners, journalists, warders and shysters in **Roxie Hart** and Madeleine Carroll in **The 39 Steps**. Most of all I remember Paul Baumer's outstretched hand at the end of **All Quiet on the Western Front**, an image that has influenced my life and my work and haunts me to this day. **All Quiet on the Western Front** is an example of what Bruno Bettelheim called a good movie. This is a film that presents:

> ...situations and ideas that induce the spectator to re-examine his life and its purposes. Out of...(this) experience, he may arrive at spontaneous new decisions about himself and his way of life, decisions that awaken in him, or encourage him to persist in, the elusive search for meaning and the widening of his consciousness of freedom.

The cinema has been condemned throughout: from the start of moving pictures, through the invention of sound, and the development of television and video. Over time, audiences have fallen and cinemas have closed. It did seem terminal in the mid-eighties when fewer people were going to the pictures per year than once went every week.

It has since bounced back with the multiplex - the dream palace of the 1990s. The opening of Britain's largest multiplex in Bristol in August 1994 shows the confidence cinema has again, in this city at least. As we approach the centenary of cinema next year its survival and prosperity seem guaranteed.

Many dislike the films and experience of cinemagoing today. Often is the accusation made 'they don't make them like they did', frequent the statement 'we used to go every week, now we can't remember when we last went'. Such comments are present in some of the contributions to this book.

These longings for a golden age have always been present. It will be said in fifty years time about the 1990s as it is said now about the thirties. And perhaps it is true. Cinema is predominantly for the young and each generation will see and prefer different films. My own favourite moments noted earlier - and most of my favourite films - are from a different period to the present. But life moves on, the movies move on - and I still go: each time the curtains open I feel a little happier than I did before; and each time they close I think about coming back again.

Note

For further information on the cinema and the audience see:

Breakwell, I. and P. Hammond (eds) **Seeing in the Dark: A Compendium of Cinemagoing** (Serpent's Tail, London, 1990)

Talking Pictures: The Popular Experience of the Cinema (Yorkshire Art Circus, 1993)

Kaufman, G., **My Life in the Silver Screen** (Faber and Faber, London 1985)

Halliwell, L., **Seats in All Parts: Half a Lifetime at the Movies** (Granada, London, 1985)

Chapter 1

A Boy in the Stalls

Wally Ball

Dedicated to my two children, Edward and Kathleen.

'Send the kiddies to the pictures,
Father's coming home today.'

This little ditty was sung during the war years of 1914-18. Soldiers were coming home on leave, wives had not seen their menfolk for quite a while, lost time had to be made up. 'Send the kiddies to the pictures.' Yes, I remember it well.

From 1908 to1916, 35 cinemas opened in Bristol. I lived in Redfield, in an area called Moorfields. My favourite local picture house was the Globe at Lawrence Hill. Saturday afternoon was the children's matinee. The entrance fee in those days was one penny. We had to throw our penny into a fire bucket by the red plush curtain at the entrance. A local lady, Mrs Harriet Brain, stood by the bucket and when she heard the sound of metal drop, she would let us go through the curtains and into the picture hall. Next door was a metal scrapyard, and many children would climb over the wall, get scrap washers and throw them into the bucket. The penny-in-the-bucket system did not last long because soon there were more washers in the bucket than pennies. The children were not stealing the washers, only borrowing because the scrapyard belonged to a Mr. Pugsley who also owned the Globe!

The inside of that auditorium left a lasting impression on all who entered. On the two side walls from the front to the rear were beautiful hand-coloured paintings about 8ft. square, depicting the Great Fire of London. Many of the Bristol cinemas had hand-painted murals.

The Globe opened in 1914, and when it was built, it was said that Mr Pugsley the owner remarked that he would like to see it burn down. Quite an odd statement, but quite understandable. Mr Pugsley was blind, so if he was able to see it burn down it would mean his sight had been restored.

In those days films were silent and subtitles were flashed on the screen so the audience could follow the story. Many people could not read, so they would take someone with them to read out the captions. It was quite normal to hear a murmur of voices during the showing of the film coupled with the pianist tickling the ivories. There is one thing I must mention. It is the 'smell' of the old cinema. As soon as you stepped into the picture hall, it was there. I cannot describe it. It was not unpleasant, it was pleasing. It gave you a feeling of being somewhere you wanted to be. You liked it, it was inviting. I wonder what happened to that smell? I suppose it is gone with those picture houses of yesterday.

In those early days women wore long skirts. Some swept the floor. One day, watching the queue going into the Globe, a lady said to me, 'Do you want to go into the pictures, sonny?' I replied, 'Yes, please.' She lifted up her skirt and said, 'Get under here and walk in with me.' I did not accept her offer. I never did like confined places.

Further up from the Globe was the St. George's Hall in Church Road (later called The Granada). It had only one projector and when one part of a film had been shown, which was about 20 minutes, we had to wait five minutes until the other part was fitted. Children would get impatient and start stamping their feet and throwing orange peel or apple cores at the screen. It was bedlam. Further up the road was the Park Picture House. Many happy hours were spent at these places.

When the Great War 1914-18 ended decorations were hung across the road from the Globe to the terraced houses opposite, and a large white sheet with the words in black paint, 'Welcome Home Mr. Johns'. He was the manager of the cinema and very popular with the patrons. He had joined the army at the outbreak of war and was now coming home. In the next street, Dean Lane, now called Russell Town Avenue, were decorations across the road celebrating the end of the war, and hanging down was an effigy of Kaiser Bill, the German Emperor.

Yes, I enjoyed going to the pictures. Picture shows were so much a part of our life in those days. There were the serials, always adventure stories.There was one called **The Perils of Pauline**, starring Pearl White. Those serials would leave me biting my finger nails. Pearl White would be tied to the railway track, the train would be speeding along the line towards her. She would be struggling with a look of terror in her eyes (the pianist all the while, running frantic fingers up and down the piano keys), when suddenly on the screen would flash, 'To be continued next week'. Another time she would be seen being lowered into a vat of boiling oil. She always survived. It was a sprat to catch a mackerel. We were the mackerels and would save our coppers waiting for next week to come.

The cowboy films, the comedies were all good clean fun. My favourite cowboys were Tom Mix and Buck Jones. When we were playing in the streets we would imitate the good guys, not like today when it seems the bad guys are the good guys. The comedians, Harold Lloyd, Chester Conklin, Fatty Arbuckle, Harry Langdon and of course our 'Charlie', the unforgettable Charlie Chaplin. I remember him in a film, **Shoulder Arms**. There was a song at that time to the tune of 'Redwing'.

And the moon shines bright on Charlie Chaplin,
His boots are cracking for the want of blacking,
And his baggy trousers they want mending,
Before they send him to the Dardanelles.

I remember another film of his, **The Kid**. It was in that film that a child actor named Jackie Coogan rose to stardom as the waif adopted by Charles Chaplin. Yes, Charlie was the King of Comedians. He was a little vagrant with his bowler hat and boots that were too large, baggy trousers, tight jacket and of course his swinging cane. As soon as he appeared on the silver screen the audience would start laughing. Local shopkeepers would pay to have an advertisement flashed on the screen before the start of the film or between shows. It was a usual sight to see a man pushing a cart along the roads and on the cart would be two large boards with posters pasted on, advertising the film being shown at the particular cinema that week. Yes, there was great competition in those days amongst cinema proprietors. Most of the cinemas were independently owned. There were permanent boards all over Bristol advertising the various cinemas and their goods. In the cinema foyer were cabinets for the display of photographic 'stills' showing scenes from the film being shown.

I loved going to the pictures as a child but very often did not have the money. Most children have their fantasies. Mine was saving Mr Pugsley from some danger he might encounter, and as a reward he would give me a free cinema ticket for life. Little did I realize that the 'free ticket' would one day become a reality, but that is a story I will tell later.

When I grew older, in the early 1920s, I spread my wings and started going to picture houses in nearby districts. There was the Vestry Hall in Pennywell Road, the Gem in Broadweir, the Magnet in Newfoundland Road. Many of the suburban picture palaces were called 'Bug' houses. Dazzling lights outside, but rather questionable inside. More often than not when you came out you would start scratching. It was so cheap to go to those places. The highest priced seat was sixpence. They would shut a blind eye to anyone taking in food. Fish and chips, pork bones washed down with lemonade. Some of the older patrons would finish with a bottle of beer. They were poor districts and it was 'anything goes'. Going to the pictures made folk forget about the squalor and unemployment at that time.

The Globe had an orchestra and, before the start of the film, the violin and the string section would tune up with the piano. When you heard that sound you knew any moment the film would begin. Suddenly the lights would dim and slowly fade out. All the chattering and nattering would subside into silence. The audience would be taken into a world of 'make believe'. When the performance ended, a picture of King George would be flashed on the screen, the orchestra would strike up with the National Anthem, 'God Save the King', lights gradually come on full and the doors flung open with a crash, and amid a murmuring of voices the audience would go out into the world of reality... Wonderful days.

There was pathos, excitement, adventure. To the queues of people waiting outside all this was available on the silver screen. The young, the old, mums, dads and young lovers holding hands. Homes were very poor with no central heating and certainly no television, but inside those picture halls there was warmth and comfort.

In 1923, I saw a 3-dimensional film in colour. As you went into the cinema you were handed a pair of cardboard spectacles. One lens was coloured red and the other green. As you looked at the screen with the specs, the picture became 3 dimensional, lifelike. The picture was of multi-coloured fish swimming around and lasted about five minutes.

There was a cinema I went to in the early 1920s called the Olympia in Captain Carey's Lane just off Old Market. It later became the Tatler. It cost three pennies to go into the Olympia and sometimes you would be given a free comic. In Old Market, the barrow boys would be selling all kinds of goods. Fruit, sweets, toffee apples and ice cream. For one penny we could buy a large bag of 'pinky' fruit (apples, oranges, etc. that were beginning to go off) to eat while watching the film. The cores and orange peel with sweet wrappers and other things would be thrown on the floor. You can guess what a mess there was to be cleared up at the end of the day. Maybe that was part of the smell I mentioned previously.

On NewYear's Day, l925 about 1,700 children were let loose within the walls of the Olympia cinema. It was the sort of bedlam that one rejoices at, for every child was the son or daughter of a man who died on active service during the 1914-18 war or who had died since as a result of war service. It was a treat made possible by the generosity of the proprietor, Mr S. Justin who gave the children a two-hour programme of films, absolutely free of charge. After the showing the children were entertained to tea by the Bristol and District War Committee.

Cinemas were not allowed to show films on Sundays, but some held free concerts of local talent and a voluntary collection for charity was made. Some of the acts were very good. At the Globe there was a rope blocking off the gangways. These ropes were at various intervals from the front to the rear. They were there to separate the different priced seats. Two pennies in the front, four pennies in the middle, and six pennies at the rear.The further back you sat from the screen the clearer the picture. The toilets were at the the rear of the cinema, if anyone in the cheaper seats had 'the call of nature', they would have to duck under the ropes to reach the rear to go into the toilets. On the way back some children would sit in the higher priced seats and not go back to the cheaper seats in the front. Sometimes they would get away with it but if the attendant spotted someone doing this astonishing crime he would get hold of the culprit by the scruff of the neck and return him to the cheaper seats. My neck used to get sore very often.

Man in the box

Yes, those were the days. The picture houses of yesterday had certain peculiar virtues of their own: their cheapness, the length of performance, comfort and a veil of darkness which could be very convenient.

In March, 1927, on leaving school at the age of 14, I went out into the world of unemployment and poverty. After a couple of menial jobs, I had an interview at His Majesty's at Eastville. There were seven other applicants for the post of assistant operator. I was the last to be interviewed and got the job. My salary, fifteen shillings a week.

I had to report to the Metropole at Ashley Road. I was met by the chief projectionist, a Mr Tommy Stone, who shouted out to someone who was in the room above, 'Bill, put this young lad through his paces'. With that, I had to climb an iron ladder which was attached to the wall leading up through a hole in the ceiling and into the operating room, bare walls and stone floor about 12ft x 6ft.

That afternoon, looking through the porthole windows in the operating box and down upon the people watching the film, I suddenly realized I was now on the other side, no longer the 'boy in the stalls' but the 'man in the box'.

One evening, a fortnight after I had begun working at the cinema, I was in the rewind room next to the projection room. This was where the films were rewound so they could be shown again. Suddenly there was a loud clatter of grinding metal. I rushed into the projection room. The film had broken on the projector (a common occurrence in those days) and was jammed in the picture gate. The heat from the arc lamp had set the film on fire. The chief was trying to put out the piece of film with his cap. I rushed over and stamped on a piece of burning film that was on the floor. We succeeded in our efforts and within a few minutes the show went on. The manager complimented me, saying 'some young lads would have panicked and run away'. He increased my salary by sixpence. It was at that time I realized why the chief wore a cap while working in the projection room. It acted as a dowser if the film caught fire on the projector.

Man in the box - Wally Ball

In July, 1928 a 'Super' cinema was opened in Castle Street. It was called the Regent. It had all 'mod cons', a mighty Wurlitzer organ that would rise from the floor and the organist would play to the audience before the film commenced, and also in the interval. It had 2,050 seats and standing room for 212, café and cloakroom. Their first showing was a silent film, as talkies had not arrived in Bristol at that time. This was **The Magic Flame**, starring Ronald Colman. The Regent was only a few hundred yards away from the King's in Old Market.

People flocked in their thousands to go to this posh cinema. The price of entry was the same as the King's. The King's had been built in 1911 and could not compete with the grandeur of the Regent, attendances at the old cinema started to fall. As a gamble, the King's was wired for sound in 1929, and in March opened up with the talking film, **The Singing Fool** featuring Al Jolson. Yes, Jolson brought sound to Bristol. I had an afternoon off from my job at the Metropole and decided to go and see and hear these 'talkies'. It could be my future. When I arrived, there was a queue stretching from the King's to the top of Old Market. It cost me sixpence to go in. As I sat waiting for the film to start I felt a feeling of expectancy amongst the audience, at the prospect of something wonderful, something magic. The lights slowly went out and the film began.

Al Jolson had left the hospital where his child, 'Sonny boy', had died. But the show must go on, and Jolson went back to the theatre where he was appearing as a coloured singer and started to sing. On the screen was a close up of Al Jolson with a picture of his little boy superimposed, smiling and with his hands outstretched. With tears rolling down his cheeks, Jolson was singing,

The angels grew lonely,
They took you because they were lonely,
Now I'm lonely too Sonny boy.

That was the end of the film but instead of the

operator (he must have been sadistic) bringing the lights up slowly he switched them on full. I looked around.There was not a dry eye in that audience. Women were crying, men were wiping their eyes. When I gazed on those faces I said to myself,'The talkies are here to stay.' The audience loved it. When people first saw moving pictures they could not believe their eyes. When they heard the talkies they could not believe their ears.

The film was shown for five weeks, four shows a day, and every performance was packed. The gamble paid off.

In March 1930 I was transferred from the Metropole to the Eastville Hippodrome at Stapleton Road. The cinema had been wired for sound. I believe it was the first cinema in the suburbs to go 'talkie'. I was promoted to chief projectionist. The opening film was **Broadway Melody**. The sound system was sound on disc (record) which had to be synchronised with the film. Many complications occurred. Sometimes the needle on the disc would jump a groove and the film would go out of synchronization. The sound would come after the person on the screen opened his or her voice. The film then had to be stopped and that reel of film started all over again. Sometimes, by carelessness the wrong disc would be put on the turntable, much to the amusement of the audience and an admonishment to the culprit by the manager.

On one such an occasion during the showing of a war film the disc put on the turntable belonged to the reel of film which showed the battle scenes. When I started the film and disc the picture flashed on the screen was making love in a hay field but instead of romantic music there was the sound of cannon fire, shrieking of shells and exploding of bombs. After a while a new system was installed with the sound on the film, and life became more bearable.

By mid 1931 all of the cinemas in Bristol had been converted to sound and silent films started to come to an end.

During this period of 1927-38 I worked at five cinemas, the Metropole, His Majesty's, Eastville Hippodrome and the Carlton at Westbury-on-Trym. I also showed films at the Bristol North Baths in Gloucester Road. In the winter, boards would be fitted over the pool and projectors fitted in the room at the rear. At His Majesty's, they had double seats in the balcony. Looking from the portholes of the projection room, I could clearly see the two back rows. Some of the scenes I saw in those back rows were more exciting and interesting than the film that was being shown. A handy man was employed at the cinema who would do any repairs needed. He spent more time repairing the back seats in the balcony than any others in the cinema.

One day a colleague of mine who was dedicated to his job told me he was leaving the business. His wife had been 'playing around' while he was at work. For cinema workers there was no normal social life, long hours working every evening and during holidays. My friend realized that to save his marriage he had to give up the job he loved. That was one of the hazards of being a cinema worker.

At the outbreak of war, all cinemas were closed but within a week they were opened again. It was decided the cinema would be good for morale and to show propaganda films.

During the war many women undertook skilled jobs that had previously been carried out by men. The first woman projectionist in Bristol was a Miss Ellen Perry, who became a trainee at the Odeon, Broadmead in 1939.

In the face of television, between 1949 and 1976 thirty cinemas closed their doors. Some were converted into bingo halls, others were bulldozed and food stores built in their place.

Nearly three quarters of people who go to the cinema to-day are under 30 years of age. Young people have grown up with television and find the big screen exciting. Older people watch their films in the comfort of their homes with a mug of tea or a glass of beer in their hand.

Looking back on those days as 'the boy in the stalls' I remember cinema as the magic carpet that took me to a fantasy world of laughter, fun and adventure. Then as 'the man in the box' I helped to create that dream world for other people. There was no greater thrill than to see a packed house transfixed by the images projected on to the screen.

My schoolboy fantasy to be given a free ticket also came true; firstly by watching all those films as a projectionist and later as an honorary member of the 'Cinema and Television Veterans', which means that today I have a free pass that entitles me to go to any cinema in the country.

The magic of cinema has never dwindled and although television and video have brought mass entertainment into the living room, cinema audience figures are growing once again. The big screen, the excitement of viewing with a large crowd and the unique atmosphere of the auditorium live on.

Chapter 2

Saturday Morning Rush

Our request for memories of the Saturday morning cinema for kids brought in shoals of replies. Here is a selection:

Tom Mix and co

Mum says. 'Get the shopping done and I'll give you a penny for the pictures.'

So I gets on my horse, and gallops off to the butcher's. On the way I shoots Fatty Arbuckle. He's teacher's pet, and a sneak. He goes for his gun, but I beat 'im to it. I'm the fastest gun in the Ole Kent Road. Hitching me nag to the lamppost I enters the bar.

'Give me a shot of rye,' I orders. The butcher says,

'What?'

'Arf a pound of sausages,' I explain. He wraps up the dogs, gives me a mean look, and says, 'That a be thruppence.'

I shoot him as well. Just before he dies he says to an old dear waiting to buy her dripping, 'The kid's bonkers.'

'They all are,' she says. So I shoot her too.

I bolt down my dinner and am out the door as fast as you can say Tom Mix. Down at the pit door the kids are waiting. They have been there an hour. 'What kept you?' says Billy. 'You'll be late for your own funeral.' I push Billy. He pushes Ginger. Ginger lands on Arfer. Arfer can't do anyfink. He's the smallest. 'Sides Ginger is sitting on 'is face.

The doors open. We all get wedged in the doorway. We unscramble and give our pennies to the old dear who is sitting knitting. Then we scramble through to Wonderland.

The film starts suddenly. We cheer. It stops. We boo. Throw monkey nuts and orange peel. Charlie Chaplin flashes onto the screen. Good ole Charlie. Always gets the best of the bullies. Then follows a film about a soppy girl who always gets 'erself tied to the railway lines or a barrel of dynamite. Her boyfriend is soppier than 'er. Don't matter how much we stand on our seats and point out that the villain is behind him, he still gets bashed on the head and tied up; but he gets away and dashes off to rescue his sweetheart. He takes a long time, so does the train as it races along the same bit of track and unless we come next week we never know whether she gets run over.

Rin-Tin-Tin the wonder dog comes next. He does a better rescue act. Finally our favourite, Tom Mix, who shoots the villain, that is the one with the black hat and is unshaven.

We go out into a world that doesn't understand dreams. We mount our steeds and ride off into the sunset.

Derek Ewer

Saturday at the Park

It was the same every week, a process of extracting a few pennies from my mother, father, or any other gullible relative with promises of work on tasks that would never be started, let alone completed, to get enough money to go to the Saturday morning cinema at the Park Picture House in St George.

I would set out with a few friends and pick up others on the way. We laughed, skipped and fought our way along the pavement, growing in number and speed at every street corner until finally an army of children marched into the foyer. The entertainment started with a film which was either a simple good versus bad struggle or an amazing adventure where brave children overcame impossible odds.

As the glow of the main feature faded there was just time to get an ice cream and settle down before the cinema manager came onto the stage to whip up the excitement level by announcing that he had achieved a miracle in obtaining a large number of cartoons. He would start by saying, 'Not just one cartoon,' followed by a loud cheer. 'Not just two cartoons, 'even louder cheer, 'Not just three cartoons.' The cheers could now be heard three streets away. When he reached six we were all hoarse for the rest of the day.

I was captivated by a serial with a spectacular aeroplane crash in the jungle. The children survive and have to make their way back to civilisation. The crash made such a vivid impression on me that when asked to write a story at primary school, I set out to repeat the events of the plane crash as dramatically as possible.

My description had everything, lightning dancing on the wings, the turbulence of the air, the plane thrown around the sky, and of course the brave captain fighting against impossible odds. Suddenly a mountain range looms up. The captain has to jettison fuel to reduce weight so they can fly over the mountain. The plane loses too much fuel and the captain is forced to land in the jungle.

I wanted to describe how the fuel was getting low and, knowing little of aeroplanes, but something of cars, I wrote, 'There were only two gallons of petrol left'. To my horror the teacher picked on this point to ridicule me and my story in front of the class. He painfully explained that aeroplanes didn't use petrol but aviation spirit and needed hundreds of gallons not two. The class laughed and laughed at my expense and so a promising literary career was brought to an early end.

Next week I was back at the Park cinema and both the teacher's words and the children's cruel laughter were soon lost on me as the magic of the cinema took over. This time, however, my cinema going had gained a new dimension. Perhaps I couldn't spell aviation spirit but perhaps, just maybe, I could prove the teacher wrong by becoming a film producer and filming the frantically spinning dials as the plane lost height. This thought sustained me until I had to give my full attention to saving the world from the evil emperor Ming and his death ray.

Dave Thorne

Gone in a Flash

Flash Gordon! That was my favourite. The weekly serial was the high point of Saturday morning at the Rex in North Street, Bedminster.

Chucking of sweet papers, gobs of chewing gum preceded it. Kids were noisy and impatient once Woody Woodpecker had done his turn and been replaced by a second rate black and white 'B' that had too many 'soppy' scenes for juvenile tastes.

It was the serial they'd come for, left in a cliffhanger from last week.

The chucking stopped, cheers and yells were directed with ear splitting excitement as Flash appeared, tights unblemished by the raging inferno he had leapt through to aid Dale who had been sentenced to some horrifying ordeal in order to persuade her to marry the dastardly Ming. No pre-marital sex in those days!

She was the only 'soppy' we put up with, a spur to Flash's heroic deeds and therefore imperative to the storyline.

Spielberg would have laughed at the reptilian monsters that Flash had to contend with. But we didn't. They were the high spot of the film, huge, roaring but a bit jerky in movement.

Flash passed with the sixpenny entrance fee for the ABC minors. He was sadly missed. Zorro,

Raiders of the River, - even the Men from Mars failed to fill the gap.

The sixpenny rush had become the ninepenny rush, and the bus fare back from the London Inn to Glyn Vale had risen from a penny to twopence. Inflation and television had arrived.

For me, the golden age of cinema ended there. The wide screen and the dare devil adventures provided by the serial were being superseded by the telly, that black and white bug-eyed screen inside a little wooden cabinet with doors on the front. The Coronation spawned loads of them, if I remember rightly.

James Bond revitalised that sort of excitement in my teens and early twenties. So, in my middle age has Indiana Jones. But nothing can compare to the excitement that started the minute you walked through the door of the Rex, smelt the mix of disinfectant and jelly babies, and clapped your eyes on the plush red velvet of the old style picture palace. And all for a silver sixpence.

Jeanne Allen

Maxine Davies of Horfield recalls the atmosphere of these Saturday morning audiences. She remembers more about them than about the films themselves.

'... the Whiteladies cinema full of kids twittering like a vast flock of starlings. Much banging of seats until the programme began, mock battles and an occasional earnest fight. Crunching and crackling of chocolate wrappers underfoot and rustling of popcorn bags.

'...Children sitting downstairs were watchful of the audience in the balcony, dropping chewing gum on to unsuspecting heads below. Children in the row behind were inclined to kick the seats in front of them, especially if bored by the film.

' ...There was a boy named Clifford I met at Saturday morning pictures, back in 1949, when I was nine years old. One day we caught a bus up to the Downs after the programme. Somewhere near the White Tree, he draped his raincoat around his shoulders, fastening it at the neck with one button. I thought this was the most dashing arrangement I'd ever seen. "You're the nicest boy I have ever met", I told Clifford. He smiled modestly and whirled round like Superman.'

Albert Johnson laments the passing of the cinema of his youth:

'When we were young my sisters and I always had an argument with dad for the money to go to the threepenny rush News theatre each Saturday morning to see Dick Barton, Jock and don't forget Snowy and the Drango Kid with all the cartoons as well. We all lived in a dream world then. I regret having to grow up but that's a fact of life that nothing stands still.

'That's where most of what I know comes from - going to the cinema. When we were old enough to start work my two best mates and I lived in the cinemas. We went seven times a week, sometimes more if there was a good film on somewhere. In those days if you wanted to find your way about town people would tell you the way by going from pub to pub and we did the same, but from cinema to cinema. There was not a lot to do in those days but go to the cinema. There was no television and the radio was not much better. Of course there was Tommy Handley or Bill Cotton. If you did not like - or have the courage - to go dancing or spend your life in the pubs, you went walking or spent your time in the land of dreams like a lot of us did.

'I have not been to a cinema for many a year now. It's not the same any more. I wish it was. The people were much friendlier then, not like it is today. You try to speak to someone, they ignore you or ask you for money. Most of the films that we saw in those days showed you the difference between right and wrong.'

TOM MIX
Comes to TOWN!

Chapter 3

Flea Pits

For every Clare Street Picture House, Regent or Triangle among Bristol's posh cinemas there were the less salubrious, neighbourhood 'fleapits'. But they conjure up affectionate memories nonetheless.

The Gem Palace

This place is fixed firmly in my mind, as where I first saw 'moving pictures'.

On temporary licence from the Eye Hospital (late 1928), I was indulged by my father, so naturally I tried everything I thought I could manage. I'd heard older lads talking about **The Charge of the Light Brigade**. Claims like 'Thur's millions of dead men - an' 'orses - too. We musta killed millions'. Blood and thunder, though I didn't know exactly what it meant, I felt I would enjoy it. Others were sceptical,'Thass all malarkey', they maintained. Probably, but I was hooked already. So I tried to get father to take me to the Charge. He gave in as always.

'Right,' he said, 'the Gem Palace t'is then.' Now because of my injured eye I was not supposed to read print etc, but the silver screen as I had been told, would present no problems.

The next evening he took me through Cheese Lane and on to Tower Hill, where trams swirled down to the Ha'penny Bridge, all was magic. When we reached Old Market, Castle Street, Castle Ditch and the Star Coffee House, I was in a wonderland of lights and movement. I'd spent a long time in hospital, I never saw anything like this.

Down Castle Ditch to the junction of Broad Weir, Narrow Weir and Philli-I-fi Street. I felt safe with my Dad, but I wasn't certain how he felt. This was the Promised Land, the electric lights of Old Market behind us, I was in the realm of ancient gas-lit shops and narrow alleys. The seventeenth century building of Taylor and Low's - bombed 1942 - was a perfect model of a gingerbread house, but real. I felt the magnetism of Bygone Bristol, which has never left me.

We passed the windows of fascinating shops, tea rooms, a chip shop, odd trades like furriers (fur merchants), to a wide open door leading to a plush lined hallway which father called a foyerr (Bristol for foyer). There was Red Plush, the epitome of elegance. It was like a picture (a still life I had seen of Buckingham Palace; the King was lucky to live in a place like this; could he go to pictures any time he liked, I wondered?)

In the foyer was a fat shiny man, garbed like a tin soldier, his brass buttons shone, his cape hung like a spare handkerchief, he looked the man in charge. Dad spoke to him. He peered disdainfully and grunted, 'The gallery entrance is around the cornah - Merchant Street. Hit's the wooden door next to Dale's 'noos hagency.' He sounded very important - amongst that red plush.

We passed the furniture shop on the corner of Merchant's Street, and turned in. There was the small wooden door, right where he claimed it was, plastered with programme adverts making it look like part of the 'noos hagency'. Dad pushed the door, it scraped open and we entered a covered passage with an earthen floor.

It was very dimly lit by an oil lamp, in the corner I could see an open staircase resembling a builder's ladder. This worried me, heights affected my balance. Father strode towards the ladder. He made me go up the ladder, admonishing me not to look down, I didn't, I daren't. Suddenly I found myself on a balcony with rows of wooden seats; the Gallery.

A film had ended; a new one was being loaded. So the lights were turned up. The place was half full, all males. On the stage by the screen, a pianist was tinkling away at wartime melodies, creating a MARTIAL MOOD for battles to come. As the lights faded for the main show, I saw the small group of boys next to me were from our own district. Under control of a no-nonsense big brother of thirteen, they sat glued to their seats. He, the escort, offered to lead me through the action. It being understood next time we met I would share my goodies with him. It was fair, father would surely fall asleep half way through. Talking during silent films meant nothing apparently, because anything verbal would come up on the screen in sub-titles.

The Gem

I remember the thrill of the cavalry charges, they went on for hours, charging left and right. I knew the British, they had square tops to their helmets.The Russians looked villainous, wore leather knee boots and had beards. Identity solved, what were they fighting about? Then my learned friend tried to explain Romantic Interest, to a group of would be Lancers, who thought girls 'soppy'.

It was to do with Plans, which the hero carried around with him. A dark lady (obviously a spy, or vamp) slipped from room to room, spying furiously. The Lancer followed her to snatch his plans back. A huge Russian, complete with sabre and battle axe, sprang out of a wardrobe to brain our hero.The Russian lost; the hero gave the plans to our side, who charged the Russians. In the mêlée, men in kilts fired at anything in sight, whilst playing mute bagpipes. That bit was noisiest as the piano player substituted for the sounds of battle. All the survivors (our side) went home. I thought for years that Balaclava lay in St Paul's and the war was because a Russian had pinched papers from us, and we wanted them back.

One thing puzzled me for years. When they towed the guns, or carriages slowly, the wheel spokes turned forwards, when the horses galloped with the guns the wheel spokes went the opposite way to the vehicle's progress - odd that. When talkies came the Gem began to slide. It became a boxing hall until a young boxer, Jimmy Cooper, was killed by falling on his chin during about...The Gem seemed jinxed, it became a store. In the 1960s it went with the slum clearances. My last sight of the Gem was when the foyer was a blank space between two shops, waiting demolition. The main hall stretched behind two other derelict shops; tatty decorations still clung to the auditorium walls.

Like so much else the Gem has gone, but somewhere, for a few years yet, will be some like me, who saw their first pictures there. And have not forgotten the magic.

Benjamin Price

Memories of the Gem from Mrs L. Davies

'In 1930 I worked in a transport café a few yards away in Merchant Street, where a passage between two shops led to the gallery up some rickety stairs.

'This "flea pit" as we knew it, was very small, with wooden benches nailed to the floor to stop them being stolen. It cost 2d, and as I earned 3/6d a week, it was a real treat on my day off.

'The films always seemed to break, and while we waited for them to restart, we would stamp and boo, just like the kids.'

The Vestry in the 1920s

The Vestry Hall in Pennywell Road held about 200-300 children every Saturday morning. It was a hall with a flat floor, just one small stage about 20 feet by 20 feet, rather a platform. The screen was above this platform.

The projector was situated in a small hut, like a garden shed, at the back of the hall in the main gangway.

Most of the seats were separate, so the kids moved around just where they liked. When the light of the projector was switched on, dozens of kids would jump upon the small stage, and for about fifteen minutes the place was in uproar. Some were trying to make funny silhouette shapes with their hands, while the rest of us were pelting them with 'pinky' fruit. The noise must have been heard on Stapleton Road.

In the first film - a cartoon, the Ink Man - someone starts drawing from an ink bottle a man's face, which moves all the time, then his body, legs and so on until he is complete, doing all sorts of funny tricks. Next, Felix the Cat, years before Mickey Mouse. Then up would come a sheet of music - 'The Little Brown Jug' - a ball bobbing up and down on each word, the lady at the piano keeping time, while everyone was yelling his head off.

Now for the Big Film - Zorro with his black cape, hat and mask, but most of all, his bull whip. Douglas Fairbanks, jumping from one roof to another, sleek black hair and his little moustache. He was a Man's Man. After seeing Zorro, all the kids next day were little Zorros, whips made from straw ropes used on crates of oranges, plaited together. Great days.

Now for Pearl White tied to the railway line, express thundering down, all steam and black smoke. It is almost upon her, bedlam, boos and shouts from everybody. 'Continued next week.'

Monday night is mum's and dad's night out to the cinema. Always a weepy, with nasty husband, drunk, beating up wife and children, no food, clothes or fire in the grate, wife forced to take in washing, falls ill, kid taken away and put in a home. Mum always comes home from the cinema crying, but still with a few cough drops left.

Thursday sees a change of programme. Moby Dick, with Lionel Barrymore chasing the Big White Whale, as big and wide as the street we live in. Our hero rows out in his small boat, the huge monster turns and attacks him, smashing the boat to pieces and tearing off his leg. They cauterise his stump, our eyes popping out of our heads, and they make him a wooden peg leg.

Years go by. He swears his revenge. Out searching, the cry goes up 'There she blows', he's found Moby Dick, and again they set out in the rowing boat, his harpoon strikes home, but again the whale turns and wrecks the boat. This time, our hero hangs to the rope attached to the harpoon. Hand over hand, he pulls himself towards the enemy, urged on by hundreds of voices, through the water at 60 miles an hour he is dragged. He climbs, with peg leg and all, to the whale's back, slashing with his large knife.

Cheers and shouting erupt around the hall as our hero has won.

'There she blows' could be heard for days after. The lady at the piano certainly earned her keep that morning.

The **Keystone Cops** was one of the best films shown in my day. The Cops dashing down the main street in a Ford lorry, a dozen or so all sitting upright. The tram cars moving towards each other, the lorry goes between the trams, comes out the other side, squeezed to half its size, but twice its height, the cops still sitting upright, still chasing the robbers.

Then there was Harold Lloyd hanging from the clock arm over a busy street 200 feet below. Yells from the kids, with everyone on the edge of the seat, stamping and shouting. Just as well they were silent films, we kids made the sound, with the lady at the piano. Everyone would be yelling 'Look out, he's behind you', or 'Look behind the door'.

The Vestry Hall, Magnet, Gem, Olympia, were mad houses on Saturday mornings. Tonight, mum and dad off to the Vestry, my brother and sister are all out, so mum takes me along. She carries me in, no charge for child in arms. War film, **Over the Hill**. Two brothers, one in the German army, the other a Yank. The German one shoots his Yankee brother, then carries him home to mother dying. My mother and other women in the cinema are sobbing, with dad tut-tutting. Dad was at Ypres, Mons and the Somme. How did a Yank get to the Western Front? The war was over before they came into the trenches. We're back to 1914/18. I never asked his views about the second war. He was a home guard. I was doing the fighting.

Fu Man Chu, Bulldog Drummond, Tugboat Annie, Charlie Chaplin, Buster Keaton, Mary Dresler, Tom Mix and many more were shown in the little flea pits as they were called.

To get the money to see these films, many errands were run, jam jars collected, old socks, wool only, take them along to Roses the scrap yards in Lawford Street, for a few pence. Money was hard to come by.

I'm sure the advertisement, the Bisto Kids originated from someone seeing us kids coming out of the Vestry Hall on Saturday mornings. There's lots and lots more, sorry if my memories don't make a good story, but it's the way you tell it, so put the blame on me.

B.N.

1937

I was eight years old, one of six children with working class parents, and we lived in Hill Street, St Paul's. In those days, going to the pictures meant a great deal to us kids as it was an inexpensive two hours of entertainment.

We never had much going for us in working class St Paul's. There simply wasn't enough spare cash to go round.

There were approximately thirty cinemas in Bristol, with a couple of variety theatres showing films as well. We were spoilt for choice, but stuck to the cheapest and closest venue. The nearest was the Magnet cinema in Newfoundland Road, and I well remember the deafening cheers from the kids for 'our boys' during a Tom Mix or Buck Jones cowboy film. There were plenty of boos for the bad guys. Known as the 'penny rush', the Magnet sometimes welcomed their young audience with a small bag of free sweets.

No free sweets in the Vestry Hall cinema in Pennywell Road, though, just the possibility of some free fleas. Some good serials were shown here, such as **The Clutching Hand** and **Flash Gordon**. It was annoying, however, to be left in mid air when one episode closed right in the middle of an exciting scene.

On two occasions my two brothers and I ventured out to the cinema on Wells Road, Totterdown. To get there we took a tram car ride from Old Market.

We went once to the News Theatre, top of Castle Ditch but found it cost twice as much as other cinemas with programmes of only seventy five minutes, showing newsreels and a few short cartoons. We felt we hadn't had our money's worth.

The Empire Theatre showed films on occasions and one film they were due to screen was the **Lives of the Begal Lancers**, starring Gary Cooper and Victor McGlaglan. We decided to go to see this film because it sounded good, and it also meant a feast. The afternoon came and we set off. First we walked up to Woolworths in Castle Street and bought a penny bag of 'bits' at the sweet counter. The big bag of 'bits' contained damaged bars of chocolate, stuck-together toffees and trodden-on various sweets.

Then we walked back down to Old Market and the Bristol Bakery shop next door to the Empire. There we bought a penny bag of 'stale 'uns'. A number of stale buns and cakes. We had plenty to feed our faces on as we watched and enjoyed the film. We watched the film through and my brothers said they were off home. I liked the film so much I stayed on to watch it through again.

I arrived home some two hours late to receive a strong ticking off, sent to bed without any supper. But I didn't mind as I was full up with buns and sweets.

Leon Paice

Mr A. Bayly is one of many Bristol people to remember the Redcliffe cinema, on Redcliff Hill opposite Guinea Street, the site now of a block of flats.

'It was a "fleapit" that held a few hundred patrons, but gave good value for money if one didn't mind seeing older releases from the city centre cinemas.

'One attraction was the slide that appeared on the screen during the interval, with a crinolined lady surrounded by flowers and the announcement that the cinema would now be sprayed with "June" perfume. On cue, an usherette would walk up the centre aisle with a flit gun spraying left, right and centre with this obnoxious odour. Anyone seated near the gangway was covered in the stuff, which stayed on their clothes for quite some time.

'The appearance of the slide on the screen was the signal for the young men to up and away to the toilet to avoid contamination. In those days, the macho smell for men was tobacco or carbolic soap.

'But it was a popular little cinema, sadly missed by us regulars when it was destroyed in one of the blitzes.'

Lipstick Kisses

They breathe all over each other
in the hot smoke dark of the cinema -
he tastes of Bourneville chocolate and hope -
- and she tells him: a child
grows in me like vines.

On the screen, a woman
stretches along a sofa,
reads magazines, decorates
her toe nails, eats boxes
of soft-centred chocolates
then shuffles to meet her lover
in scuffed sling-back slippers
shedding fluff.
She is - all lipstick kisses
and tar-blacked starfish lashes,
a cloud of talcum powder
and scented wrists.
Half-woman, smudged out,
muted, a woman who is
barely. She lifts herself
onto her toes to reach his cheek.
White steam curls off the tub

and he shaves in broken mirrors,
cracks his face a hundred ways
says being with her is
like having cream with everything
says: love is eternal.

In the claret-coloured dark
of the half-empty cinema,
the man in the under-stuffed
back row seat
says: impossible.

In the foyer,
a geranium drips petals
like confetti, lipstick red
while his words fall around
his girlfriend's shoulders
like broken glass.

Rosalyn Chissick

Film Star - Gregory Peck

(où sont les neiges de Kilimanjaro?)

imprinted
as a gosling to a goose
how could I fail
to choose him?

Gregory!

tall, dark, divinely serious,
hesitant;
rich gravy voice -
I had no choice.

- an accessible mix
of my father
and Prince Charming -
he provided an emotional fix;
disarming,
and, since repeatable,
always reliable.

able,
with that profile,
and the dear mobile
muscle in his cheek,
weekly
to make us weak
in our soft plush seats -
Margaret and I.

He could deliver,
twice-nightly,
predictable casual charm
which made us shiver
deliciously,
and sigh....

A film star
doesn't let you down.

On that great screen, far
above,
he need only clone performances,
re-enact known motions,
to confirm devotion,
love:

and probably wreck
thereby the prospects
of a real life claim by any male
less practised; scripted;
plain.

I can't complain.

Imprinted as I began,
I met my own lead man
similarly tall and dark
and slim;

and,
Reader,
I married him.

Nadine Vokins

Chapter 4

Courting Days

Like thousands of Bristolians, **Bert Richings**' 'first date' with his wife-to-be was to see a film. He recalls that evening at the Eastville Hippodrome in 1935, where they saw **One Night of Love**.

'It was 'Bon-fire Night' and during the show someone threw a firework into the gangway. When it went off, it frightened the life out of everyone in the cinema. We have always said our love life started with a bang.

'Most of our courting days were spent in cinemas around Bristol, the most popular being His Majesty's at Eastville. One night, I primed myself up with two of each kind of fruit that would go into my pocket, unknown to my young lady. During the film, we became so hysterical and caused such a disturbance that we were asked to leave, which we did. Were our faces red!

'... The coming of talking films put fresh life into the industry. It was out of this world to actually hear the stars speak, and of course Al Jolson was one of the first of the singing stars, with 'Sonny Boy'.

'What was so handy was you just looked at the entertainments page in the evening paper, picked out the film you most wanted to see, and jumped on a tram-car for a few coppers. Most districts had at least two cinemas, changing films twice a week, so the choice was fantastic.

'We will never forget those good old black-and-white days, with the words appearing on the screen and the old piano tinkling away to the tempo of the film, going mad if there was a chase or a fight, or slow and gentle for a sad, or a love scene.'

The cinema played a big part in **Doreen Bolt's** life. She remembers: 'I was 18 years old in September, 1938. Having returned from a week's holiday in Southsea, I was at a loose end and my mother suggested I go to the pictures. It was a Monday evening, and the place, the Stoll Picture House in Bedminster.

'A young man was going in at the same time. The usherette asked "Double?" I quickly said no, a single, but she did seat us together anyway. During the interval Ivor, this was his name, offered me a cigarette and although not a smoker, I accepted. Incidentally, he never offered me another, as he really didn't like women to smoke. Anyway, he walked me home, and although perhaps not love at first sight, it was instant attraction.

'Ivor really was tall, dark and handsome. Being 5ft 10ins, I was conscious of my height, which has never bothered me since. It was one of the happiest days of my life, and we were engaged the following May and married on September 3rd, 1939, the day war was declared.

'....I have been on my own now since 1977, but I have a lovely family, three sons and daughters-in-law and six wonderful grandchildren. It all began on that day in September, 1938. We always enjoyed the cinema, and as a young family in St. George went regularly to the Park Picture House, often twice a week, and also to the Granada.'

Jan Bebbington started late. 'It was to do with mixing with the wrong children and being shut up in the dark. My mother didn't want the former and I couldn't bear the latter. Here I was at eight, still sleeping with the light on and the door open so that I could see everyone as they necessarily walked past my room to bed. My cousin hindered my development when he locked me in the garden shed, leered through the window and related tales of blood running down the picture house aisles and the usherettes wading around in boots.

I eventually got to the cinema by the ingenuity

of my friend who wrote a note in her best handwriting to my mother. "Can Janet come with me to see **Around the world in eighty days**? We will be home by five. It's my birthday." It wasn't but I went, armed with a present. We ate the box of Maltesers before Pearl and Dean had a chance to flash across the screen.

'Jeanie was an old hand. We sat at the back and watched the fourteen year olds snogging. Any older, she told me sagely and they come to the evening showing, dressed to the nines on arrival and minus various pieces of underclothing when they left. I didn't understand.

'We skived off school for **The Sound of Music**, missing hockey and lukewarm showers. We sang all the way through, making up what we didn't know. We wept at the end stopping only when we met the cold light of day through the fire exit and saw our bus vanishing past the library.

'I had a torrid affair by post with a vicar's son. We met outside the Gaumont and the following week we met again but didn't see much of the film. When we weren't necking, I was keeping his hands from under my skirt and vowed to wear trousers next time. He went to university. His letters were lurid.

'When he came home the following term, I waited underneath the advertisement for the following week's films and wondered if I'd recognise him. I did and he limped. Have you hurt your leg? I asked and then realised that one was shorter than the other. We both blushed and rushed into the dark, enveloping comfort of the cinema. We saw **The Music Lovers**. "I adore Tchaikovsky," he sighed. "So do I." His arm shot around my shoulders. The lights dimmed. I shrank with embarressment as Glenda Jackson thrashed about in an overtly sexual manner, displaying armpits which were exceedingly hirsute.

'Video couldn't compare with the cinema even with curtains drawn and popcorn tumbling to the floor. There were no icecream drips or love-bites from home viewing.

'On our wedding night we hired **Amadeus** and settled in front of a roaring fire. The dog slept across the hearth, nose working like bellows. We ate a takeaway from foil trays and the film clicked itself on. I remember nothing and slept through it all. Dream on...'

Under the raincoat

Meg and Tom were born in the late 1920's, growing up during the second war. At the time the blackout was in force prohibiting all street lights and no chink of light was allowed to be shown from any house. Cars and public transport were cut to a minimum due to the lack of petrol and oil. Food was rationed so 'eating out' was rare and very expensive. Social life was in consequence, limited. There was, however, a ray of light, the cinema, albeit only open for three evenings each week.

It was a life-saver for Meg and Tom. They would make a bee line for the Oriental cinema, or flea pit as it was known locally, and weave their way through the strategically placed curtains. These hung so that none of the foyer lights showed outside as the audience was admitted. Then they held their breath. Had Percy, the man in the ticket office remembered to reserve their double seat on the back row? Yes he had and they made their way to their familiar places and sat down trying to look pure and innocent until the auditorium lights went down. Unlike many cinemas the Oriental sported three double seats on each side of tbe single central aisle, and they were always in great demand. It was amazing what contortions could be performed without the restricting central arm.

Some of the films were in black and white but many were in colour, considered at the time to be very new and exciting. This did not matter to either of the youngsters who were literally wrapped up in each other. Even such stars as Alice Faye, Jane Russell, Lynne Barrie, John

Payne, and of course, Glenn Miller who was at the peak of his success at the time, couldn't hold their attention for long.

However Betty Grable took the biscuit. She of the gorgeous legs, reported to be insured for a million dollars, at the time an unbelievable amount of money. Not only this, she was married to Harry James the handsome trumpeter, and he was always worth listening to. Fred Astaire and Ginger Rogers flitted across the screen and Rita Hayworth added a unique glamour to any picture in which she starred. Esther Williams was different though! She cavorted in the swimming pool with a perpetual smile upon her face, which made one wonder if it was painted on by some photographic genius. All these stars sang and danced their way across the silver screen while heavy petting was carried on under the cover of the darkness and the use of the raincoat, always carried, winter or summer, and regardless of the weather and the quizzical looks of parents.

The only trouble with not watching the screen or bothering to listen to it, was that one was taken completely unawares when the lights were switched on at the end of the first house. They would suddenly flash on, causing a lot of scrambling and straightening up of clothes. Boy friends were left with their faces covered in lipstick.

It was difficult to look totally innocent and calm within seconds of the lights coming on but Meg and Tom found their technique improved with practice. This was of paramount importance on a Saturday evening as there were often many neighbours and friends of Meg's parents visiting the cinema.

The first house watchers having left and the second house audience seated, the lights would dim again. Movietone News would then be shown, heralded by the crowing of a cockerel and Lesley Mitchell's voice speaking as though he was in a race and the audience was suffering from impaired hearing.

Pictures about the war and the great successes of our troops in North Africa and Europe would be shown, but ignored by the young couple. After all, there was only about two hours left of the evening and it was not going to be wasted by looking at the screen.

Maggie Hughes

Here's looking at you, Albert

As time goes by, our memories fail us. Names and dates grow hazy and recent events soon fade to grey. But flashes of the past remain. As clear and constant as they ever were. More real than reality. Shivers of a summer's night in 1943 when I was seventeen...

In the space of two hours, I fell in love twice. First with a handsome young airman called Albert. And second with Humphrey Bogart. Or was it the other way around? I'm not sure.

But I do remember the Galaxy Cinema, dark and airless, wisps of cigarette smoke rising to dance with dust motes in the funnel of light from the projector. And Bogart and Bergman in **Casablanca**. Who could forget? Lovers divided by a divided world. As Albert and I were soon to be divided.

I wept for Ilse as she stood by the piano while Sam played 'As Time Goes By'. And then for Rick when he saw her there, his mask of world-weariness crumbling away to expose such raw emotion I don't believe there was a dry eye in the house. We knew what it was to endure the suffering and sacrifice of a senseless war. Our hearts went out to them, willing them to find a way, not only for themselves but for each and every one of us. But it wasn't to be. Like us, they were at the mercy of influences beyond their control. The plane took off leaving Rick behind and, as the credits rolled, Albert pulled out his handkerchief and tenderly wiped away my tears.

Two days later, he was gone, posted 'Out East'.

I went to the station to see him off, smiling bravely, yet all the time wondering whether I'd ever see him again.

The sheer joy I felt when he was finally demobbed was indescribable. All our hopes and dreams were fulfilled and life was ours at last. We were married before the year was out. Three lovely children in quick succession completed our happiness.

I'm a great-grandma now. And a widow. My Bert's passed on, and so has Bogart. But I'm still in love with them both. I always shall be. And however much time goes by I'll never be able to watch **Casablanca** without shedding a tear.

Tina Wade

Chapter 5

Extras

No one bothers me

I can remember cinemas I've been to, I can remember films I've seen, but rarely can I tie the two together, remember facts in teams. Perhaps this is because the viewing is supreme.

I go to cinemas, so that the space and blackness will grant admission to the concoction of luminosity before my eyes, losing me in illusion, for a brief two hours' rest. And the illusion being all, I prefer to go alone.

For years, I've gone alone, no distractions, no commenting female friend, no groping male, not even a carton of popcorn. Alone.

Over-fearful female acquaintances can't get over this. They cluck and shake their heads, stare at me in horror. 'We couldn't go by ourselves,' they say. 'We might be bothered.' Meaning men. And so they go in gaggles, or with husbands, boyfriends, friend, or watch a video at home, missing the true relationship with artefacts of light. They don't believe me when I tell them no one bothers me, in middle age, with greying hair. No one bothers me.

For the most part, this was always true, at afternoons or early evening shows, at respectable cinemas, in the better parts of cities. Yet I remember that once it wasn't so, and it's the cinema I see, the film's forgotten.

The entrance was an archway from the high street, set between two shops. Then a whitewashed stone faced tunnel, like the horses' entrance to a coaching inn, led to the multipaned glass door fronted foyer. In a minor Midlands town, the cinema was small, in need of renovation. I chose my seat with care, many had been ripped and stained beyond repair. It was well patronised. A film, presumably, that 'everybody' saw. I didn't take much notice, when a man slipped into place beside me, but soon I was aware of him, shifting, getting comfortable, I thought, until an arm emerged from the shadow of his person and laid itself along the back of mine. Alert, I waited for the next move. It didn't come, so I left it where it was, the arm, and it became companiable with time. And so we stayed, dim figures to each other, faces never seen, gazing at the screen.

It was before the end, before the lights came up, he asked if I was coming, if I would leave with him, and I said No, I wanted to watch the credits. In a normal voice, politely. And so he left without me, straightaway. The shadow left, average in every way. Even the voice, I'd never recognise again.

This happened many years ago, the cinema's long gone, but the image lingers, black and grey, a scene played in a pale reflected light, a curio of no importance. It doesn't bother me.

Anne Edwards

Glamour - 1940's style

The film was **Samson and Delilah**. Hedy Lamarr lay on a sofa draped in lamé and Victor Mature, to whom she fed luscious black grapes. Later the handsome Victor demolished pillars with the touch of a finger. In the utilitarian 1940's this was glamour!

I was twelve years old and watched entranced on three successive evenings until my mother found out and forbade me to see it again.

That wasn't my first taste of cinema, though. Our Boxing Day treat was a visit to the pictures, usually to see Errol Flynn swashbuckling his way through **Robin Hood** or the even more dashing **Captain Blood**. 'Who's your favourite film star?' was the question on everyone's lips at school as we eagerly related the adventures of the night before. My sister fell victim to the dark and smouldering charms of James Mason. I preferred Orson Welles and we argued fiercely over the merits of our respective idols.

Our local cinemas were The Granada [now a Bingo hall] in Church Road, St. George, and The Globe at Lawrence Hill. In those days you could expect to see two films, a newsreel and the forthcoming attractions at the very least. There was the main feature and a supporting 'B' film, often a cowboy, in which Ronald Reagan chased Indians relentlessly, or a mild detective story. It was all grist to our mill and, armed with a shilling bag of sweets, we settled down happily for several hours of escapism.

Occasionally we ventured further afield to the posher town cinemas like the Odeon or the New Palace [later the Gaumont] in Baldwin Street. These cinemas had their own cafés, so we enjoyed a little of the high life before seeing the film, eating large quantities of toasted tea cakes and eclairs oozing artificial cream.

I saw **The Way to the Stars** at the Odeon, memorable for the sixteen year old Jean Simmons singing 'Let Him Go, Let Him Tarry', and a poem by John Pudney entitled 'Johnny-Head-in-Air,' which I can remember to this day. It paid tribute to the role of the R.A.F. in war time and we wept copiously, treating ourselves to fish and chips from the shop in Carey's Lane afterwards.

Inside the Regent cinema

Carey's Lane, of course, was the home of The Tatler, well-known to Bristolians for its screening of what were regarded as slightly naughty films and unfairly believed to be visited only by men wearing dirty raincoats.

Cinemas were well-patronised then and if you queued for the 1/6s at the New Palace you could often exchange greetings with friends in the 2/9s as the queues snaked round the block and met in Clare Street.

How exciting - and innocent - it was. We dreamed our dreams and were none the worse for the notions of bravery, courage and faithfulness we imbibed so eagerly.

Gill Sheppard

Golden Age

I started visiting the cinema regularly in my teens, which was for me the golden age of cinema. I shared the view with my friends (and still do) that the cinema was the best thing since sliced bread. Living in a sparsely populated village where nothing much happened, an evening at the cinema was always looked forward to and planned to the utmost detail. This was the social event of the week, the time for the ritual washing of hair, smartest clothes (tightest jeans and smallest t-shirt), mascara, eye liner, blusher and lipstick (strawberry flavour) to be applied to full effect yet sparingly enough to be allowed out by my eagle-eyed mother.

Apparel approved, I would meet my friends at the bus stop and wait for the country bus to ramble its way to town. Eyes blithely turned to each other discussing the latest film to be seen, reviews passed on by word of mouth from others who had seen it, how frightening it had been (I was going through my horror period). Arriving at last at the cinema I can remember tumbling out of the bus anxiously scanning the queue already forming. Who was going tonight, anybody we knew, anybody we could join? If the queue went past the fishmonger, you knew there wasn't a chance of getting in.

In at last, entrance fee paid, packets of sweets and drinks in hand, we would climb up the dark stairs, hand the usherette our tickets and walk down the dimly lit aisle trying to find the best seats. Impatiently we would watch the documentary that was always shown first, a captive audience for the local adverts that followed next. Then with the first half over and the interval concluded we would all settle at last for the eagerly awaited feature film.

I can remember to this day watching one of the Friday the thirteenth films and screaming at the end when the hand suddenly erupts out of the water and grabs the boat. I never lived that down, it scared the hell out of me and for many weeks after I checked when my parents had gone to bed that they had securely locked and bolted the doors!

Watching on video many years later the same film I was astounded that it had so much impact on my life then. It certainly scared me out of my craving for horror films. This I can only put down to the special atmosphere that is created by a big screen and being part of an appreciative audience.

Sue Williamson

Flashback

I'm sitting in the cinema. Seat at an angle. I expect the previews, but the picture in my head appears instead. The six other Monday night people think it is the big film.

There's my dad, the film star, and me, the sidekick, taking a greyhound for a walk. Early Ealing studios perhaps, or maybe John Grierson. Black and white. We pass a heap of rubble on some waste ground.

Life is hard for us in black and white. Our house was condemned before the war. Damp and infestation fit for heroes. My mother cooks on one iron ring that swivels over the open fire. The production values are tight. Her dream is to have two iron rings so that she can worry some stew and boil potatoes at the same time. This is so authentic! Life on a raw, broken-glass edge of a wall, with nothing worth stealing on the other side.

The black and white flickers into colour tints. For on this waste ground there grow a few lupins. Purple spikes that drain to yellow and then cream at the tips. The picture flickers. The sound falters, grey, out of focus, out of sync. All seven of us stamp our feet. I look round at the other six. Whose film is this, anyway?

The picture clarifies. The words are still lost in pre-Dolby time. Does someone speak? 'Let's pick some and take them home. Nobody will mind.' Who says that? Does my dad read his script with feeling? 'Your mum will like these.'

Maybe he thinks the two rooms are so dingy, a gas mantle glowing desperately onto the central fly paper sticky with flies, that a few flowers will brighten up the place.
What is the motivation here? Coal mining - dangerous - dirty - poor pay - demoralising - here is a free gift of nature.

Does he think he can make amends for the nights my mother and I, as a four year old, turned the sharp corner into the dark, empty, midnight street, wishfully thinking that this was the moment he would return from his drinking and womanising. Perhaps the director wants an act of kindness here. Remorse.

Film promotion outside the Tatler cinema

Audience reaction - wet popcorn.
I cry tears for the boy that was me - the boy who needs protection from the harshness of his script, from the absence of love in his method acting. I need this man, this Kirk Douglas chin, this Robert de Niro darkness to say : 'Let's pick these for your mum.'

Even at that age, the child star knows that people have flowers in their houses. He has heard it on the radio or seen it in a cartoon at the Palladium.

The scene is re-taken, re-edited, like some false memory. Get it right. I can't stand this. My chair flips up. I move back a dozen rows. The cinema has emptied, this is better. I hear more clearly.

FATHER: I think they're called 'Lupins'.

BOY: Take one home for mum.

FATHER: (Pulling back on greyhound's lead) Don't be stupid.

Jim Edmiston

Le Cinéma Français

In Spring, 1970, and after working in France for several months a friend and I decided to complete our education and go to see a French film.

We buy the small magazine which lists events in Paris and scan the pages. We have heard of many, mostly American imports, but to see one of those seems to be defeating the object, and cannot decide which to choose. In the end, we look for a name which seems vaguely familiar and find Francois Truffaut's **L'Enfant Sauvage** (The Wild Child).

The cinema is in the north of the city, on one of the wide boulevards. The day is hot, the traffic noisy, and the cool darkness of the cinema is a welcome change from the clatter outside. Not knowing what to expect, we wait. We have heard about French cinema. Very arty, contrived, obscure, evocative, a contrast to most of the films we had seen until then and probably completely unintelligible (even if we can understand a film without English sub-titles) to anyone from the country that produces **Carry On** films. No doubt it will have something in common with the Impressionist painters - misty focus, clear light shining through the leaves. To be analysed and discussed in detail.

Then the film starts. I can still remember the shock of that moment. The rather grainy black-and-white film can only mean low-budget and probably inferior. My heart sinks as I feel the disappointment that we will have wasted an afternoon of glorious sunshine by visiting the cinema. Still, as we do not have much money and we have paid, we stay.

Without wishing it, I become completely absorbed by the story. Set in the nineteenth century, the village doctor is told of a child being found in the forest and who seems to be half-animal, moving around on all fours, only making grunting noises. The doctor and his housekeeper take the boy into the house and try to clothe and feed him, though the boy fights their attempts, kicking, biting and squealing his fury.

Gradually, they start to communicate using gestures and basic language, but the boy remains a mystery. No-one knows where he came from, how he got to the forest, nor how long he had been there. Visitors come from far away to see this strange creature, who does not seem to be troubled by extremes of temperature and to have existed for so long like an animal.

It was so long ago. Have I remembered the story properly? I'm not sure.

The film finishes. We sit in our seats, stunned. Still in a nineteenth century village in rural France we slowly leave our seats in the cool greyness. Wordless, we make our way out.

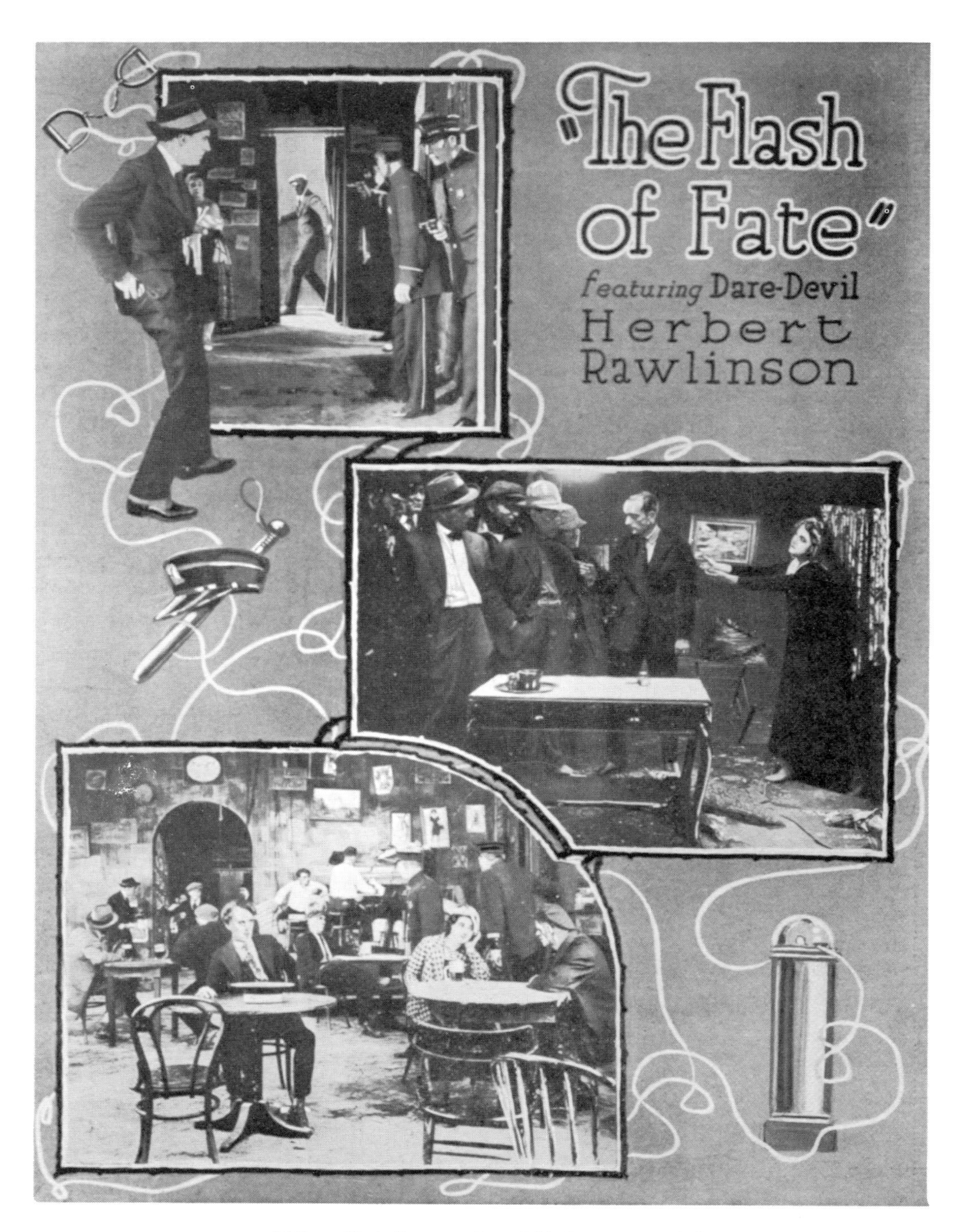

Film distributors' publicity material

The colours, heat, noise, smell and dust hit us like a bombshell. We look around, astounded that that world is still there, another real world. It had been so different from our expectations: no mist, no light through leaves, no analysis or discussion. Too important for that, too striking.

Janet Burke

The window

It's only a few steps from the grey light to the warm enveloping blackness. It's different in there.There's a window to the world that should have been his, and for a while he'll be safe.

He is surrounded by them. The ordinary people. The people who belong in mediocrity and anonymity, and he resents them being shown his world.

He moves with them to the rows of seats and he's glad that no one speaks to him. What could he have to say to them? He sits and stares straight ahead, waiting for the window to open.

Behind him a girl giggles. He hears the rustle of clothing as she moves closer to her boyfriend, but he doesn't look round. He knows what they are doing and, just for a moment, he wishes he had someone beside him to touch. Then he remembers. They're ordinary and he's not. He doesn't need ordinary people, and it's not his fault he is trapped with the common and mundane, adrift from where he should be.

The window to the other world opens. He shifts uncomfortably in his seat and wonders why he doesn't have the house or the car or the girl or the life before him. He shakes his head, not understanding, and whispers, 'It should be me, it should be me.'

And then the golden hour passes. Suddenly he's no longer the one in front of him. He is there, through the window. Everything that happens, happens to him. And if he just reached out, he could touch the players around him. When the girl says, 'I love you,' she says it to him. When there's gunfire it is he who runs from cover to save the day. He smiles and knows it is a winning smile.

And then it's over. The lights go up, the music fades and he is swept along with the tide of ordinary people, out into the grey light again. He stands on the litter filled street and shakes his head as people pass by not noticing him.

Why don't they know? Why don't they see he doesn't belong with them? Why don't they realise that it is only some strange quirk of fate that condemns him to a life without family, friends, job or money? Why don't they see that he belongs through the window in that other world?

He looks at the poster advertising the feature soon to open. He sees his own smiling face and his name in bold print but knows he is the only one who sees it.

'Never mind,' he whispers.

Only a few days and he'll be back through the doors and into the world where he belongs.

Tony Domaille

Thursday

Hello again. Yes I'm back risking disappointment or wonder with another unseen film that I know nothing about. Can't even remember, let alone pronounce the title, so I always ask for 'one, please' and spend the eternity after feeling embarrassed at my perceived ignorance.

Step up to the grill and it's the same old faces, the same old hunt for the card, the desperate hopeless scramble for the right money as the queue behind me shuffles its feet and mutters (maybe) about the time I take before I collect my thoughts, collect my ticket, collect my change, smile and step away.

I don't know anything, except that today it's raining outside and dry and so exciting in here. Coat drips over the programme notes as I wait outside trying not to lose my ticket in the couple of minutes before I have to go in.

Still, here I go again, old familiar seat, as uncomfortable as ever, hopefully to be soon forgotten with this afternoon's trip to... somewhere. Somewhere else that isn't here, I don't even care if it's raining there too; just so long as it's nothing I've seen before.

Clothes are beginning to dry now, damp cloth scent and I'm trying to figure out if I'll be dry by the time it's time to leave, when the lights dim like a promise and the ads kick in. Recite the tag lines and add your own dialogue. Wait, wait, like a child before Christmas and the trailers add their own tension, hints of presents to come and soon it's over. Now it arrives, lights go down further and I leave my Thursday behind, dripping and sullen, and I'm into somebody else's life, sucked through the screen, clothes and seat and life forgotten.

Time passes, marked with swift furtive glances to the clock; wanting to know how long it is before I have to stop living, get back to the drab reality that's starting to stab me from below. Shift, move, lean forward, anything; just don't lose your grip on the screen in front of you, don't stop looking, not for a second.

But I can't hang on forever and things resolve themselves (or don't) and they all live happily ever after (or don't) and the lights come up again, stern parents and it's way past my bedtime and time to go. One last check to see if I've left something behind (any excuse to come back) and it's out to the rain again, clothes following clammily; streets grey, no longer Technicolour. Say goodbye, nod your thanks to those familiar strangers and hope it's maybe just "au revoir".

Duncan Keen

Chapter 6

Gaiety Days

Denys Chamberlain

The magic, the glamour, the excitement of the world of movies. The premières, the glitter, the stars, the world of make-believe, but was it all like that?

I was brought up in the magic world of the 'picture house'. My father and grandfather were both involved in cinema exhibition; I had an uncle who accompanied silent films on the piano, another who designed and hand-painted cinema posters for most of Bristol's picture houses, and yet another who was a cinema manager. We all lived in the glamorous world of moving pictures and my contemporaries at school before the war marvelled at the fact that I could go FREE OF CHARGE to one of my father's cinemas every night of the week without seeing the same film twice. Yet on a Saturday afternoon my best friend's father would take myself and his son to the Regent in Castle Street and would have to pay for me!

One of my earliest jobs in the cinema was to rewind the films up in the 'operating box' - I was so short that I had to stand on a film transit case to reach the rewind bench. Later, I was allowed to scratch out the slides shown to advertise the following Sunday's feature film. This involved coating a piece of slide glass with a paint-like substance and, when it was dry, using a sharp instrument to cut the letters. It took a long time and often they were finished at school. Was it any wonder that my school work left much to be desired. Yet it all came to my rescue when in my School Certificate examination I received a credit for the essay that I wrote.

The essay? What else but a description of the basic workings of a cinematograph projector. My earliest memory is of listening to a 'sound picture' shortly after the installation of the equipment at the Knowle Picture House, together with the marvel of hearing my mother reciting poetry through a microphone in the operating box whilst I sat and listened in the auditorium. What an experience - I could hear my mother but I couldn't see her!

The next thing which I clearly remember is standing at the back entrance of the Knowle Picture House on a Saturday morning holding an empty tin in which the children put their pennies whilst my father issued tickets from a big roll. **Rin Tin Tin**, a very talented alsatian, was the serial and the feature was **Alf's Button Afloat**. We gave the first children to arrive a special magic button. Showmanship at its best!

By 1933 my father had become so enthralled by cinemas that he designed and built the Gaiety on the Wells Road in Knowle and I watched with wonderment as the building took shape.

I was given a pair of dungarees and spent all my spare time 'helping' the builders. On Sundays when they were not at work, I would sneak on to the partially built stage and give 'my performance' - a vocal rendering worthy of an 'Oscar' and applauded by an as-yet unknown and unseated audience. How many millions of people were to fill that auditorium in the years to come - none of whom were lucky enough to hear my performance!

The newspaper advertisement which heralded the opening of the Gaiety on December 26th 1933 told of a cinema which boasted the latest technical developments, including 'atmospheric lighting' and oil paintings of Spanish fighting galleons on the walls, and that no expense had been spared in its construction and furnishings. This cinema was all part of the glamour side of the film industry. Money was not that plentiful and corners had to be cut. Some expense had to be spared and my father saw a way to economise on carpeting the new cinema. Bobby's store in Queen's Road Clifton was about to be taken over by Brights [now Dingles] and

Gaiety cinema

the store. The carpet was 'dark brown' with a slightly lighter shade of 'dark brown' to give a two-tone circular pattern. Many years of good service to Bobby's had not improved its uncolourful appearance but in the darkened auditorium of a cinema this was of little consequence, so a moderate offer was made and accepted. Somehow the quantity was misjudged, for not only was there enough to completely carpet the whole of the new Gaiety but also sufficient to re-carpet our existing Knowle Picture House. Not only that. Our new house next door to the Gaiety had now been completed and, to my mother's eternal horror and regret, every room was also to be carpeted wall-to-wall in the two-tone dirty brown!

My favourite toy was a wooden scale model of the Gaiety. This was my very own cinema. I later obtained an old 35mm silent projector to which I fixed a belt-driven vacuum cleaner motor and showed films at a furious rate. My films consisted of all the bits and pieces thrown out by the projectionists which I carefully joined together with film cement, old trailers, and films acquired for a few pence from junk shops in the old Broadmead Arcades. Other boys at school played with their Pathescope 9.5 mm hand-turned projectors, but I had the REAL THING. Our house included a very large cellar, part of which I regarded as my theatre. I held my own special film shows there, though for most of the time I acted as manager, projectionist, staff AND audience.

A lot of glamour was taken from the cinema at the start of the war.

On September 3rd 1939, all cinemas were closed because of the danger of crowds gathering together in the event of air raids. The closures lasted only about a week, but when the cinemas re-opened the bright lights had disappeared. The red neon signs that had proudly proclaimed 'Gaiety' were to stay darkened for five years. Those big glass doors that had opened to so many people and led them into the magical world of Hollywood were now boarded over to prevent any light escaping to the outside. The cashier who took your money through a glass window on the outside of the building, now had but a small square aperture. But the queues began to form again, eager patrons wanting to part with their 6d, 9d, 1/- or 1/3d and escape from the humdrum and hard life on the home front.

And what did they see? A feature film, a second feature (usually a cowboy) and probably a two-reel comedy starring such accomplished actors as the Three Stooges or Our Gang. And then, of course, there was THE NEWS. Pathé, Gaumont British, Univeral, Paramount or Movietone, whichever one shown was well over a week old by the time it reached the Gaiety! The news was priced on its age. Release news was the most expensive, followed by 3 days old, 6 days, 9 days, and finally what may be lovingly called 'history'.

The booking of films in those days was a great business art. All the distribution companies and producers had teams of salesmen based around the country with branches in all the major cities. Bristol was mainly controlled from Cardiff. All the salesmen would gather at the Gaiety on a Monday seeking to sell their product. Often they would have a dozen or more films, all of which they hoped you would book but

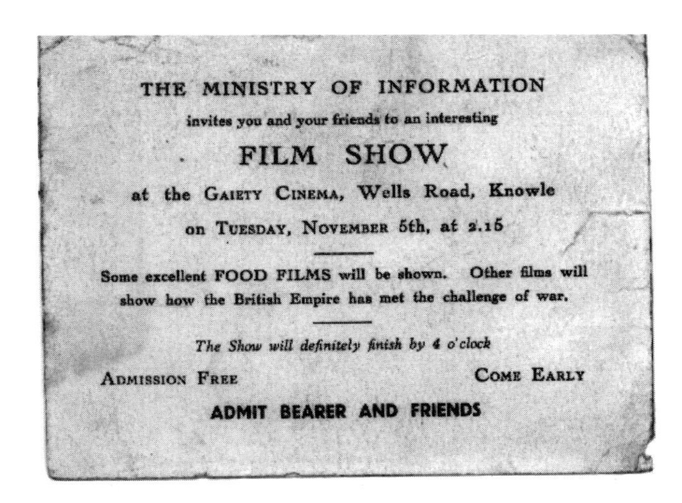
THE MINISTRY OF INFORMATION
invites you and your friends to an interesting
FILM SHOW
at the GAIETY CINEMA, Wells Road, Knowle
on TUESDAY, NOVEMBER 5th, at 2.15
Some excellent FOOD FILMS will be shown. Other films will show how the British Empire has met the challenge of war.
The Show will definitely finish by 4 o'clock
ADMISSION FREE
COME EARLY
ADMIT BEARER AND FRIENDS

book but were more than pleased if you took a quarter of them. Many worked on commission so they would set about establishing a fairly high rental which was then bartered between the salesman and the exhibitor until a compromise was reached. They would also try to achieve the maximum playing time in excess of three days for their important films.

Arguments were rarely resolved immediately and the final booking of a film could take weeks. It didn't really matter much because we were usually booked for two or three months ahead anyway. It was all 'hard sell' and a very long way from the glamour portrayed on the silver sceen.

There were many other aspects of running a cinema at that time which were far from the fascinating life of the stars. Owning a cinema involved turning your hand to everything required. When your cleaners failed to appear for work, then it was your turn to clean the toilets! I recall that we had a large hoarding outside the Gaiety which announced the current programme. On one occasion the man responsible for changing the poster was on holiday, the chief projectionist was on a day-off and all the other staff seemed to be missing or doing something very important which left no one to paste up the poster. So, balanced precariously in a strong wind at the top of a ladder, a bucketful of paste in one hand and half the poster wrapped around me, I wasn't making a lot of progress. A passer-by stopped to watch me for a while and yelled at the top of his voice, 'you never see J. Arthur Rank doing that!'

But despite the daily routine that makes any busines tick over, there really was a glamorous side to being an exhibitor. At the Annual Cinema Exhibitors' Conference you were invited to attend all the film premières; you donned your best evening attire and rubbed shoulders with the stars of the day. Crowds lined the entrances to the brightly illuminated cinema hoping to catch a glimpse of a star or two as they arrived, and even the exhibitor felt a part of that magical world.

Then there was the Royal Film Première at the Odeon, Leicester Square and the British Academy Film Awards at the Grosvenor and other events where exhibitors joined with producers, directors, established stars and young hopefuls. So, just for a short time, you lived the life portrayed up there on the silver screen - knowing that on Monday morning you might be vacuuming the stalls.

Chapter 7

Too Grand for Bingo

Many older Bristolians would claim that the Regent in Castle Street was the city's greatest cinema. Back in the 1930s most people, at some time or another, joined the thronging crowds to marvel at its palatial luxury, impressive dome and red, purple and gold interior.

The Regent boasted more than 2,000 seats in the semi-circular auditorium, with standing room for another 212. As well as a mighty Wurlitzer organ, there was space for a large orchestra. Crowds turned out just to watch the patrons arriving in evening dress for the late night performances.

Outside the Regent cinema

For many young girls in those days, being an usherette at the Regent was something of a 'plum' job. **Mrs Ida Prescott** remembers.

'It was 1932, I had just left school and was looking for work. I was offered a job at the Regent as a kiosk attendant selling chocolate. Later I became an usherette. The Regent was a very smart cinema, was managed by Mr Davis, an ex-army sergeant who treated us just like troops. We were lined up every day for inspection, our uniform was red dress with brass buttons which had to shine as did our shoes.

'The foyer of the Regent was very grand with two pay desks, white marble steps leading to the restaurant, circle and dress circle. The carpets and seats were red plush. Also there was a big lounge with tall palms standing in the windows.

'We usherettes worked in pairs, one taking tickets, the other showing patrons to their seats but we were only allowed to talk in whispers. The films were great old films, such as Gracie Fields in **Sally in our Alley** and Cecily Courtnedge in **Soldiers of the King**. One time we had a film called **Show Boat** when the usherettes were dressed in fancy costumes. **Cavalcade** filled the house to capacity. The doormen would call out 'standing-room only'. Standing-room was in the stalls where there was a big wooden barrier which people could stand behind to watch the film until a seat became vacant. It was great to hear the audience laugh at the Laurel and Hardy films but if the film was sad, you could hear the sniffs of tears.

'There was a magnificent organ played in the intervals by a gentleman, Mr Boswell, who was an excellent organist. The usherettes got to know the regular patrons, sometimes they would bring us chocolate for giving them a good seat. Courting couples we always put in the back row but the good-looking single men we tried to put in the side seats where we could indulge in a bit of flirting! We worked from 1pm to 9.30

pm one day and 10.30 pm the next, that was after "God Save the King" was played and the cinema was empty. Before we could leave we had to empty all the ash trays and turn back the seats. The manager would be standing in the foyer to see us off the premises.

'I had lots of fun at the Regent cinema. Sadly, it was lost in the bombing, but fond memories will always remain.'

Regent opulence

Like the whole of Bristol, **Mrs G. M. Haigh**, too, was sad when the Regent Cinema was lost in the blitz but thinks 'it was too grand to finish up as a bingo hall'.

'I joined the staff as an usherette in the 1930s. We wore red uniforms which matched the plush seats and decor. The cinema was always packed on a Saturday night, as they were the first to show all the new releases, and patrons stood patiently at the back of the auditorium until seats became vacant.

'The day I started, a man offered me a box of chocolates which he had purchased from the girl with the sales tray. I refused, as even in those days we didn't take sweets from a stranger. I was told later that he was quite harmless, and belonged to a local wealthy family who indulged him because he was slightly retarded. He came in every day to buy chocolates for the girls, to which the management turned a blind eye because of his connections.

'Carl Brisson was the heart-throb of the day. The word 'sex symbol' was then unknown to us innocents. I also loved the films and the singing of Nelson Eddy and Jeanette McDonald. Many promotion events were held in the large foyer, and I remember seeing Jessie Matthews there in person...When all the seats were filled, we breathed a sigh of relief and rested our arms on the back of the partition. We watched the film or the antics of the courting couples in the back row, blissfully unaware of our interest.

'I later worked upstairs in the grand circle, which you might say was 'going up in the world', as you usually got a more select clientele there. But I was intrigued by a middle-aged couple who came in separately several times every week, always managed to sit together holding hands and then left separately. Was this what is now called 'an affair?'

Chapter 8

Extras 2

Cinema alone

There was a large queue outside the cinema, and this prospect of an audience went to Fleve's head. She was plainly in one of her silliest moods, and I wished Kit hadn't brought her. When she took from her pocket a tube of bubble mixture, and started floating bubbles over the heads of the people waiting in front, I pretended I was waiting alone, and was nothing at all to do with her.

I could have been inside already if I hadn't waited for this mad lot. I could have been choosing popcorn and studying the posters with calm and dignified interest. Around Fleve, I never could feel calm.

She had begun to do her 'singing in the rain' bit down the pavement now, and everyone was staring. Only I knew that she'd copied the moves from Paddington Bear, not Gene Kelly.

She was standing now on the wall that enclosed the supermarket next door to the cinema.

'Coo!' she said. 'This is where they keep the trolleys chained up.'

I considered going home.

'People of the Western World!' she cried suddenly, and Kit groaned.

'Pity these poor enslaved creatures! By day they toil, by night they stand here shivering in chains. Is this fair? Is this just?'

There were murmurs of 'really' and 'honestly' along the length of the queue, which shuffled forward a little as if trying to leave her behind. I moved with it, as Fleve elaborated her theme of injustice, and Kit started to heckle her, playing Fleve's own game. I put my hands deeper into my pockets and looked at my feet. It wasn't as if Fleve lived near enough for it to matter if everyone thought her mad. I lived around the corner and came here most weeks - usually alone, sitting quietly in the central seats and wondering what it would be like to be sitting at the back, where the giggling came from.

Kit and I had been here together twice - but then we had both sat in the central seats, and Kit probably already knew all about sitting at the back. He only came to watch films with me when he really wanted to see the film, because I was no distraction, and I didn't need walking home. Company without complications.

I realised then that wherever we sat, once inside, Kit and Fleve would behave as if they were at the back. I really wanted to see this film, and tomorrow would do as well as today.

'I'm not hanging about any longer,' I said quickly to Kit. 'You two go ahead - I'll see you.'

I wasn't surprised when Kit made no attempt to dissuade me, but shrugged and returned his attention at once to fickle Fleve.

And after that I went to the cinema alone.

T. Kimberley

It's never too late

There was a certain inevitability about it. After all I was born in the mid Thirties - the Golden Era of Hollywood and raised in a village which could boast that its one and only cinema provided a change of double features on a Monday, Wednesday and Friday.

The result: I became a film fan. More perhaps - a devotee all but consumed with the dream to become one of the God-chosen idols 'up there' on the silver screen and frozen in time. Given the chance I too could become a movie star!

Reality dictated otherwise. Despite a brief venture into amateur dramatics my regard for my talent and ability proved to be at variance with that of the producer and I departed the scene. Suddenly the kraken awoke - for there it was in the *Evening Post*:

FILM EXTRAS REQUIRED

Major Feature Film is to be made locally during the last week of April 1980.The Production requires crowd extras for a variety of the scenes and would welcome applications from interested parties of all ages [either sex]. Please apply immediately giving details of name, address, telephone number, age, physical characteristics and availability. BOX 4063

I applied and was duly invited to a casting/costume session. I had barely entered the hall when someone shouted in my direction,'You - the tall one - you're just what we need for one of the chieftains in the Highland Games sequence!'

'Does that mean I'll be wearing a kilt?'

'Naturally!'

Two ambitions fulfilled at once!

Life 'on location' proved the stuff of which dreams are made. We earned only six pounds a day, but were fed and watered every hour on the hour plus a 3-course lunch all provided from a small van bearing the inscription MOBILE CATERING UNIT FOR THE FILM INDUSTRY. How such a tiny vehicle could leave 400 people fully satisfied had something of the miracle of the loaves and fishes about it.

By then the task of adjusting to wing collars, collar studs, the draught around the knees and 'What's worn under the kilt?' 'Nothing it's all in good working order!' remarks were all borne with equanimity as we acclimatised ourselves to 1920's clothing.

The working day was all of sixteen hours, but the time passed so quickly that I could have sworn we were in Oz. In place of the Yellow Brick Road, however, was a muddy field around which a clutch of athletes ran in one hundred metre bursts, while the one and only camera was repositioned for each new shot. The final shot, of course, had to show the central character winning.

Who was he? Who were they?

I recognised Cheryl Campbell from the 'Pennies from Heaven' series on TV, but she was the only one. Other names meant virtually nothing at that time: Ian Charleston, Ben Cross, Alice Krige - while the short hirsute fellow in the cowboy hat was pointed out to me as the producer David Puttnam.

'Who?'

'You know Bugsy Malone.'

'Ah!'[?]

The Highland Games heavies relieved their particular boredom by tossing the caber in the direction of the chieftains. We scattered!

The young lad sent up one of the hills to be filmed running along a track radioed down some three hours later for some one to bring him a jacket. Reaction clearly indicated the production unit had forgotten all about him.

The runners ran with renewed vigour. Jonathan put down his dog, picked the loud hailer and said, 'Camera-and-Action!'

'For God's sake, Jonathan, let the runners get back into position!'

'Who dares speak to our leader in such a manner?' I enquired.

'HE is the director, Hugh Hudson' a fellow-chieftain advised.

'Oh!' I'd never noticed him before - but suddenly

there he was. Then it was finished. Three days gone forever. Who would want to see a film about a couple of men who were involved in the 1924 Paris Olympic Games? What was it called? **Chariots of Fire**. The answer came almost nine months later - courtesy of the *Evening Post*.

> The Royal Film Performance this year is to be David Puttnam's production of 'Chariots of Fire', the first British selection since 'The Slipper and the Rose' in 1975.

I had maintained a diary of my three days in Shangri-la and sent it along to the *Evening Post* to see if there was any interest. There was - and they printed it. Meanwhile I waited for the arrival at our cinema. Then - it was to be - Next Week.

The envelope with the morning mail bore the motif of a scantily-clad muscleman in silhouette with a hammer striking a gong.

Too late MGM - you have missed your opportunity - Alan Powell has been discovered by the British Film Industry.

It proved not to be the case. It was a nice letter from the manager of the local cinema, which was owned by the Rank Organisation, offering four free tickets to see the film. Leaving the cinema after the showing I felt as if another of life's chapters had closed. Three days had become one point five seconds as far as my appearance was concerned, and yet it was the fulfilment of a dream and now I know it's never too late to dream.

Alan Powell

Uncle Bill

Twenty years ago, back in the pre-multiplex days, my father was the manager of a mammoth fourteen hundred seat, single screen cinema in Grimsby on the east coast. Being the manager's son I recall regularly running around the empty auditorium on school holiday mornings before the place opened for business, or sitting watching Gus the projectionist tinkering with his old German Kalee projector up in the sound-proof box.

I particularly remember the ritual of the Saturday morning ABC Minors' matinee. Every week Dad would march me in through the front doors straight past the long queue of kids, much to my discomfort.

Oi! Where are you going? You're jumping the queue!

Every week these words would spring from the mouth of some poor individual who had probably spent the last hour waiting to get in.

It was a relief to get past this and into the foyer. Dad would drop my coat off in his office and then present me with a complimentary mivee or bag of cashews from the kiosk. Soon I'd be ensconced in the half-light of the auditorium, a chevron of ABC Minors' badges across my chest. Eventually the hordes would filter in, the first ones running to grab the front row whilst others would head for the exits to let their mates in for nothing behind the backs of the phalanx of usherettes, who often struggled in the face of a wave of 'non-paying patrons', armed only with heavy duty torches.

After much jostling and kicking the back of the seat in front by all and sundry to deafening effect, Dad would pick his moment to enter stage left, heralded by the legend, "Boys and girls... IT'S UNCLE BILL! " A chorus of clapping, booing and raspberry-blowing would ensue.

Firstly he would take us through the Minors' anthem, something like:

> We are the boys and girls and we are
> The Minors of the ABC!
> (much emphasis on the ABC)
> And every Saturday we line up
> And see the films we like
> And shout aloud with glee.
> ...and so on.

There would be a weekly birthday slot, then the results of a painting competition or a live yo-yo bobbing contest. I recall one week the winner of this refused to stop bobbing. Dad had to usher him away as the house-lights went down for the first feature. This would usually be a Three Stooges short, certainly something black and white and old. Then a cartoon or two followed by a Children's Film Foundation 'epic' which usually boasted David Lodge as its biggest star.

By midday it was over; the urchin masses of Grimsby would flood out into the over-bright street and disperse.

Dad still sees some of his regulars, themselves now with young children of their own. For today's generation though there will be no Minors' matinee in Grimsby. In 1980 the cinema was split into three screens, and I'm afraid the magic went.

Jez Conolly

Quicksilver screen

'Boom', boom battleship guns. Smoke surges, lifts, and you glimpse hulls wallowing with each explosion. Naval history No, cinema history. It's my grandfather talking about one of the first 'newsreels' ever made.

Around the turn of the century, at the height of the Spanish-American War, he filmed the 'Battle of Santiago Bay' on the rooftop of a studio in Brooklyn, New York. Equipped with a washtub, toy boats and a lighted cigar, he cranked his camera in close-up while his pals blew puffs of smoke across the screen. His newsreel wowed audiences, who believed they were watching an actual naval battle - all silent, of course. He had no worries about synchronising realistic sounds. 'Boom, boom' could be printed on the screen, while an earnest pianist plugged away at 'Stars and Stripes Forever' and rows of faces stared in semi-darkness at the flickering shapes.

Illusion was my grandfather's trade. As a teenager he left England with his family, keen to make his way in the new world. At first he called himself a 'prestidigitator' and lived by sleight of hand as a showman in vaudeville. He liked to tinker with gadgets and to live adventurously. Maybe he had an instinct for novelty, too. Intrigued by Thomas Edison's work with 'moving pictures' he started to fool around with cameras, changing how they worked. It wasn't long before he counted himself a journalist, taking his own movie camera to record historic events.

As children we heard how he filmed President McKinley's assassination - he happened to be standing nearby. He told us how he filmed the Galveston flood, and the San Francisco Earthquake of 1906. These films had all been shown in cinemas around America before being stored away - but they were made of celluloid and a studio fire had incinerated them all. They became memories, stories.

Our favourite story was his adventure with Teddy Roosevelt during the battle for San Juan Hill. I can picture my grandfather now, waving his arms as if swatting insects. He would say, 'Whenever we set up the camera for pictures, the tropical bugs whined past our ears. It wasn't till later that somebody told me they were bullets.' That's how the story went. When I was little, I thought it was true. But then, when my mother was little, she thought he really did pull nickels and dimes out of the flower beds for her as she walked with him through the garden.

In 1948 my grandfather won an Oscar for pioneering work in the film industry. His Oscar is actual. I've seen him receiving it, on film.

Elinor Edwards

Chapter 9

The Dream Merchants

This way, please

Now, at the age of 74, I have memories of working as an usherette at the Odeon, Weston-Super-Mare, at the time when Odeons had the wonderful decor making the interiors so lavish and different from other cinemas. I remember the distinctive smell, the type of floral disinfectant used, really pleasant. I worked there for about five years. I was about 17, that would be around 1937-38. We wore green uniform jacket and skirt, with gold trimming, pancake berets. We used to put on our berets and curl our hair around the hat with curling tongs heated on a gas ring. Our black stockings were bought from Woolworths at 1/- per pair and were often mended and ladders over-secured with finest thread.

Our working hours were long. Starting at 1 p.m., finishing at around 11 p.m. each night with one evening off per week from around 8 p.m. That evening was spent in a complimentary seat at either of three other cinemas - Tivoli, Regent or Central - just time to catch the main film in those days. The programme consisted of one main feature, a second feature film and a cartoon and news also. Trailers for the next week's programme and of course there was the wonderful organ which rose from the depths with organist seated to play and sink again; always beautifully lit and a real feature of Odeon cinemas. Tickets were sold at the box office and the half given

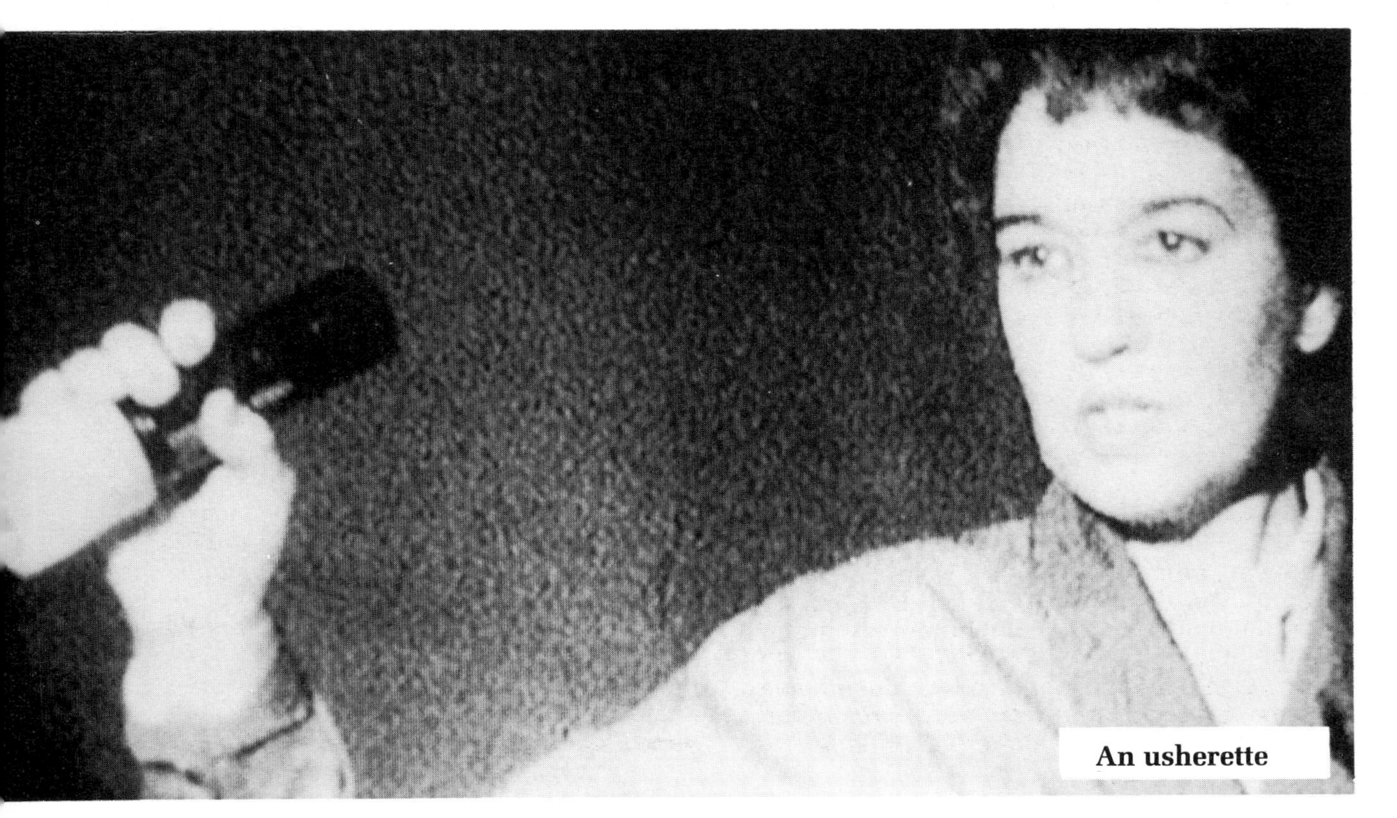

An usherette

at the entrance by the audience was threaded on to a string to be taken to the manager's office at night to tally the day's takings.

Each day before we went on duty, our appearance was vetted by the Sergeant Commissionaire, who would check hands, fingers nails, stocking seams and hair, nothing missed his scrutiny. If we had a cold it was up to his office at the top of the building for a good pinch of snuff to clear the head. It worked too...

Tea and toast was available and I remember we used to get it on a tray from a nearby hotel, The Shaftesbury, and serve it to our patrons, on request, trays collected and returned. After each day's showing, ash trays were cleaned out with the aid of a duster and dustpan and we used to curse the patrons who left the tip up seats down, so delaying our leaving dog tired and footsore after the endless torch-bearing trudge up and down the aisles.

Long queues were the norm in those days and we had to keep a constant check on empty seats and prices, to be relayed by word of mouth to the man on the door, who in turn relayed to the waiting queue, 'Two doubles, so many singles'- very welcome news, specially if it was raining.

I remember the advent of the Sunday concerts. If one volunteered to work on the Sunday evening from 7.30 - 9.30 p.m., a whole day off would be the reward. The only trouble with the Sunday concert was the showing to booked seats was done with full lights on, a daunting experience to the young and self conscious.

Prices in those days were something like 6 pence, 9 pence and 1/- in old money, of course, and my wage the princely sum of 15/- a week. To get a pay rise one would have to knock nervously on the manager's door and ask for something like half crown, 2/6.

Those were the days.

Eileen Stockwell

Mrs E. Smith started as an usherette at the Ashton cinema in 1929:

'It was quite a nice, clean, cheerful place. They opened evenings from six o' clock until ten o'clock and also a Saturday matinee. For this I was paid nine shillings a week.

'Attendance was pretty good, especially Saturday nights when one could be sure of a full house. I worked mostly upstairs, which was like two small rooms, with doors to each. Seats were mostly booked, and always young couples, who came every week, so one got to know them well.

'If the two seats near the door were booked, I knew I should be standing up that night.

'There were changes of pictures each week, besides the Pathé news. These pictures and newsreels were passed on to the Town Hall cinema and the Redcliffe, and a young man who worked with the projectionist would get on his bike to deliver them. The Town Hall was a big dreary dark place: seemed to have a lot of big posts, and if you got a seat behind one, it was a job to see the picture.

'The Redcliffe Hall was just one big hall, no upstairs. I knew the three cinemas very well, because I was sent to fill in if anyone was absent at either of the other two. I never felt happy at either, and at the Redcliffe one never knew when rats were about.

'The piano was played at each of the cinemas and the pianist followed the pictures around. So at Ashton, we saw three pianists a week. The pictures were black and white, with words coming up on the screen. Old westerns with Tom Mix, or pictures that made one weep, or comics accompanied by piano music.

'When the boss was missing, I would give the pianist a 15 minute break to freshen up or visit the toilet. I never envied the pianists their job, as they had to watch the screen for changing moods in the pictures, and play appropriate music.

'We also took turns selling chocolate: lovely bars of Frys choc, coconut bars, Turkish Delight, all 2½ d each. If we sold £1 worth, we would get a shilling which I always spent on Turkish Delight. I couldn't resist it.

'.... I used to enjoy going to the Stoll Theatre. They had up to date pictures there, with stage artistes doing turns between pictures, and also an organ. The actors always lodged with Mrs Ford who lived in Fraser Street, very near where I lived. While in this theatre, my hat rolled off my lap. A young man sitting next to me, picked it up and asked if he could see me home. We married four and half years later.'

1912, the orchestra from the People's Palace, a music hall - converted to a cinema, later called the New Palace and The Gaumont.

On parade at the picture house

96-years old **Ray Miller** was Principal Cellist with BBC West of England Orchestra and later joined the Bath Pump Room Trio.

But he started his working life before the First World War as a fourteen year old page boy at the Clare Street Picture House in Bristol. He remembers:

'It was very regimental with a 'Sergeant Major' Mr O'Halloran in charge of five men and five

page boys. Every day, at 1.30 p.m., we were all paraded for an inspection of our uniforms, gold braided with two rows of brass buttons down the front of our short coats.

'I had to stand at the top of the gangway and escort people to their seats. Before the start of the film, the quintet of two violins, cello, double bass and piano played sitting below the screen, and I had to remove the brass rails and curtains which hid them during the film. When they had finished playing, I replaced the rails and curtains. The quintet were all Germans, and of course that was before war broke out.

'When I was 15, I took a job at the Kosy Korner Kinima at the top of Union Street. My job there could be quite exhausting. Above the box office was the projection room and if the film broke (sometimes in many places after the reel was shown), it was handed down to me for repair.

'The owner had another cinema in Bedminster, called the Town Hall, and to save money on the top films, sometimes six or seven reels in length, I would, as one reel ended, race from one cinema to another with the reel on my cycle hoping I didn't have a puncture.

'Years later as a professional musician, I played at the Metropole Cinema at the end of City Road. The trio hated Saturdays, because children used to throw orange peel and sweet papers at us over the rail. On one occasion, worse happened. A drunken woman had lurched her way up to the the screen and got under the rail. She leaned up against the pianist while he was playing and peed all over his shoes, causing quite a scene.'

These evocative photographs of the Odeon Cinema, Bristol in the 1930s were sent in by **Mrs Gladys Bowley**, who now lives in Derbyshire. As Gladys Collings, she was an usherette, and took part in the publicity for **Pygmalion**. She is the one in the back of the car in the straw hat with basket, dressed as a cockney girl.

Below, Gladys pouring tea for her colleagues in the cinema staff room. She remembers these years as 'one of the happiest periods of my life'.

Embassy days (and nights!)

'The Embassy Cinema had its opening in 1933. It was the biggest in Bristol - two thousand, one hundred seats - owned by The Avenue Cinemas Company based in Wales, who also owned the Forum cinema in Bath.

I started as an usherette in 1938, a year before the outbreak of war. The hours were long and we were poorly paid, but it was very enjoyable: you met a lot of nice people and got to know the 'regulars' who used to come in every week. Before we left at night we had to tip up seats; empty ash-trays and look for lost property.

In 1939 I put down my torch and became sales lady in the big kiosk in the foyer with additional responsibility for the two sales girls, who used to go round with the trays of ice cream and sweets etc in the cinema, filling the trays and cashing up the sales. I could sit down when it was quiet - much easier on the feet! That plus the fact I could get home an hour earlier every night.

At the outbreak of the war all cinemas were ordered to close and we received one week's notice. That was on September 7th 1939. Fortunately the licence for re-opening was granted and our notices withdrawn a week later.

The air-raid shelter was one of the safest in Bristol - underground in the basement with five concrete floors above and a way out on to the pavement outside. On the night of Bristol's Big Blitz we were in the air-raid shelter with some of the patrons, who lived too far away to reach home safely. We were there most of the night, while the manager and male staff were up on the roof putting out incendiary devices.

Although that was the first of many hours we spent in the shelter we were fortunate that the cinema survived the war intact. However, when we finally did emerge on that first occasion there were fire hoses and water everywhere with fires still burning all around us. Lennards, the shoe shop, had been hit, as had the nearby Triangle Cinema and several of the shops in Queen's Road. The City Centre, of course was devastated.

We used to get a lot of American servicemen who always had plenty of money to spend but never understood its value! We had a couple of visits from a very distinguished guest, The Emperor of Abyssinia, with his wife and children. They were residing in Bath during the war.

In 1946, the cashier, who had worked there since the Grand Opening in 1933, left to be married and I took over her job. We were very busy in those days; queues all round the block. I think people came to take their minds off the events over the previous six years. The price of seats ranged from six old pence in the stalls to three shillings and sixpence in the balcony.

Mrs Fry - of the chocolate firm - often used to come. She was a very kind lady and gave me a pound note on one of her visits and a lovely jumper at Christmas. I used to receive many little gifts from patrons - boxes of chocolates etc. A very happy atmosphere always existed between staff and customers.

We had a lovely tabby cinema cat called Mitzi - after Mitzi Gaynor the film star. Mitzi was a great favourite and had the run of the cinema at night, to keep the mice away. She spent a lot of her time accompanying me in the cash desk, where she used to sit and keep guard on the pound notes I piled up until I had time to count them.

It was not only films we showed at the Embassy, we had Sunday concerts - Joe Loss and his band, Billy Cotton, etc. The stage was large enough to hold a full orchestra.

The evangelist Billy Graham also held a very

successful week with us - full houses every night. We even had wrestling bouts and a high spot - two weeks of ballet, with Alicia Markova and Anton Dolin.

There were dressing rooms behind the big stage and with the café on the second floor and the large ballroom above that, The Embassy could have made a lovely Theatre and Entertainments Centre. It should never have been pulled down; it was a great loss to Bristol.

We were all very sad as the final week approached. We had been showing a month of Greta Garbo's films and that's how we finished. Like Greta we never returned!

Elsie Pyke talking to Alan Powell

'When the red, red robin...'

My cinema memories go back 70 years. In 1924, when aged just fourteen, I was thrilled to bits to be given my first taste of the cinema world. The proprietors of the Premier Cinema at Gloucester Road in Horfield were a Mr. Justin and his son Charlie, while Miss Gregory managed the cinema and a Miss Godfrey was cashier. I was employed as a part-time usherette along with Phylis Newick, only I also had the glamour of playing piano for the silent movies every evening, and generally keeping the audience entertained until the cinema's musical trio arrived for the feature film: the Jones brothers on bass and violin and a Miss Cox on piano.

For my services, I was paid twelve shillings each week from which I was expected to purchase my own music scores. These cost tuppence (2d) per sheet from Witcombs on Seymour Road (before they moved to the Arcade) and had to be changed at least monthly so that our 'regulars' wouldn't get fed up with the same music. In those days homes didn't have television and so the cinema movie cast an escapist spell on pre-war Bristolians, which is probably difficult for today's technological

Young attendant at the Eastville Hippodrome in the early thirties

age to comprehend.

All-time favourite tunes of that year include 'In a Monastery Garden', 'Bells Across the Meadow' for the serious and sentimental and 'Moonlight Serenade'. There would be matinees on Wednesday and Saturday afternoons - the latter especially for the children when I would play 'When the Red, Red Robin Comes Bob, Bob/ Bobbing Along...' and they'd all sing aloud to their hearts' content often getting rather raucous. Eating was considered very much a part of the event and children would come armed with pomegranates together with eating pin purchased from Mr. B's shop next door.

As for myself, I preferred to have my box of dates close at hand. My consumption of these was conveniently concealed from the prying eyes of the audience by a discreet curtain lit only by subdued lights either side of the piano.

I clearly remember one occasion when just at a very exciting and crucial part in the film - which likewise required equally fast moving piano playing - I swallowed a date stone and nearly choked to death. I had to stop playing just as the film was about to reach its climax. The proprietors were not amused.

As far as the children were concerned the highlight of a matinee would be if one of the two projectionists - Charlie Belsten and George Ballard - wasn't paying attention inside the projection box and the film would jam at a vital part or - even more hilarious - the film would come to an abrupt stop at the end of reel one and the audience would have to wait in suspense for the restart of the film on reel two. This would inevitably happen just as there was some cliff hanging event about to take place or perhaps a Western shoot out. The audience would scream with laughter while a very flustered projectionist tried his best to make amends.

Dolly Westlake

'Chocolates, ices'

Mrs C. Taylor was sixteen when she went to work at the Triangle Cinema in Clifton, selling chocolate and ice cream during the intervals.

'While I enjoyed the job, it did have its hazards. We were required to walk backwards down the aisles, so as not miss the frantic waves of a potential customer. More than once, I nearly came to grief over a casual foot sticking out into the gangway, or a child running up behind.

'Another drawback was that any money short in the cash and stock at the end of the week had to be paid out of my salary. For a long time I wondered how this was happening, then I discovered from a reliable source that the manager was in the habit of plying his lady friend with expensive boxes of chocolates on her frequent visits. He was soon mysteriously replaced and everything returned to normal.

'... By the end of the week I could often recite the dialogue by heart; fine if it was a good film. Among my favourites were **42nd Street** with Dick Powell and Ruby Keeler and of course the unforgettable **Gone With the Wind**.

'Many years later, in the 1950s I ascended to the dizzy heights of usherette in the Orpheus at Henleaze.'

From page boy to projectionist

Mrs Maureen Chandler recalls the pre-war years when her father, Jack Duggan worked in the Bristol cinemas.

'He started work when he was just fourteen years old, in 1916, as a page boy at the Picture House in Clare Street. He was much in awe of the plush surroundings of this small, select cinema with only 500 seats.

'There was a pillared entrance leading to a beautifully panelled foyer with potted palms beside every door. There was a café where smart ladies 'took tea' and a smoking-room for the gentlemen.

'The page boys, all clad in smart uniforms with pill-box hats, lined up to take the patrons' hats and coats before they entered the auditorium.

'Jack Duggan later became a projectionist, working at the People's Palace (later called the Gaumont) in Baldwin Street before going to the Regent in Castle Street.

'He always spoke of the Regent with much pride and great affection, which he thought Bristol's finest cinema. He spoke of the spendour of the ornate interior, red, gold and purple. A visit to the Regent was a special night out. Castle Street was always a hive of activity, especially on a Saturday night, when the Regent always had the HOUSE FULL board out. The special midnight premières were great occasions, with crowds gathering just to watch the audience arriving, all in evening dress.

'I remember my father's projection box which was so noisy you couldn't hear yourself speak. I remember him lifting me to look through one of the little oblong windows looking down on the heads of the audience way below, and the long searchlight sweeping across them to the flickering screen.

'I also remember going with my mother one hot summer's afternoon to take him his tea. We climbed a long flight of metal steps, and sat for a while on a little metal balcony outside the projection box looking down on the ships in the harbour.

'But my most vivid memory was seeing the mighty Wurlitzer organ rising from the bowels of the cinema and filling the auditorium with its music. There were 2,000 seats in that great space, with standing room for one hundred.

'It is difficult today to imagine the shocked astonishment of audiences when, for the first time, they heard the moving pictures speak. Long queues would gather for every performance, as people wanted to witness the new marvel for themselves.

'On one occasion, my father was severely reprimanded. One day the newsreel had not been collected from the London train at Temple Meads, and my father rushed to get it himself, arriving back just in time to slot it into the projector and run it on time. I don't know if it was his job to edit, or just give the footage a run-through check but, on this occasion, he did neither. One item was the grand opening of the Chelsea Flower Show by Princess Marina. One camera was at the roadside to film her arrival. The car door was opened and, as the Princess stepped from the car, a gust of wind blew and there, for all to see, was not only royal underwear but royal thigh! It is difficult today to comprehend the consternation, but the audience gasped, and there was stunned silence. The film was never shown again.'

George Pallent's father, as a young man, was assistant to the projectionist at the Stoll cinema in Bedminster in the early 1920s.

'The projectionist had sent him out one evening to buy some chitterlings from the pork butcher's shop in East Street. Half-way through the

One of Bristol's earliest picture houses, Pringles in Gloucester Road. Known as the Scala in its later years, it finally succumbed in 1974, making way for a new block of flats.

evening performance father, who had chewed and chewed a large piece of the chitterling until he could chew it no longer, threw it through the hole through which the film was shown. Unfortunately, it hit someone on the back of the head, who in turn threw it at someone else until the performance ended in uproar.

'One of his jobs was to take the news reels as soon as they had been shown and run with them to the Town Hall cinema on Redcliff Hill, in time for them to be shown there.

'One evening, he ran, reels under arm, from the Stoll, to jump on a passsing tram, missed his step and sent the reels scattering all over East Street. That ended his career as assistant to the projectionist!'

A projectionist's tale

I am just old enough to remember the grand old cinemas of Bristol in their final days. Their names were like the constellations in the night sky, culled at random from Greek mythology, the 'Orpheus', the 'Gaumont', the 'Odeon'. Sometimes I wondered who picked these exotic names, and why, but no one seemed to know. They had always been so, timeless in their neon sky-writing, palaces of electricity and esoteric magic. Some people navigate

their cities by churches, others by pubs. At an early age I learned to use the cinemas of Bristol as familiar landmarks in my explorations of the city. I still do, even in my dreams.

In those days television was monochrome with a low definition 405 line display. The television set at home (bought by my dad for the 1953 coronation) obstinately refused to receive anything but B.B.C. Isolated from the world of 'Coronation Street' and 'Ready Steady Go' which my school-friends took for granted, I was drawn to the colour and spectacle of cinema with ever greater force. The first film I saw on my own was **El Cid** at the Scala, off Zetland Road. I didn't know then that this sad decaying flea-pit had once been one of the first and finest picture-houses in Bristol called 'Pringle's Picture Palace'.

I remember sitting in the Odeon one day in a matinee, being hypnotised by the 'beam' for the first time. A shaft of blue-white light, twisting and dancing in an aerosol of dust and smoke. I was fascinated by the eerie almost liquid quality of this high temperature arc-light which seeps around the doors and corners of projection rooms like the light of creation. For the first time I was drawn to the idea of working in the white tiled rooms glimpsed through the projection portholes, where the machines and their operators lived. In the years that followed I have spent many thousands of hours tending projectors, racing the cue dots and adjusting focus, but I still watch the light and marvel at it.

Sometimes the collision of memory and reality can be painful. I recall walking past the Whiteladies cinema when it was being refurbished and seeing the beautiful marble pillars which once graced its interior lying hacked off and discarded in a waste disposal skip. More recently as I flicked through the pages of *A City And Its Cinemas* by Charles Anderson my attention was caught by a photograph of the giant two thousand seat Embassy cinema which used to stand on Queen's Avenue (It was demolished in 1963). A matinee audience is leaving a double bill of **Lorna Doone** and **The Mouse That Roared**. In the right foreground a young schoolboy in a familiar uniform and duffle coat is walking round the corner. It was a shock to recognise myself, 30 years on.

Ewen Macleod

I Watch

I enter
I pay
I sit
I sigh

I watch
I lean
I munch
I slurp

I gasp
I grip
I fumble
I cry

I laugh
I smile
I forget
I remember

I blink
I sigh
I rise
I leave

Ann Cahill

Picture Palace

Footsteps on the pavement hurry
Fleeting past the dirtied pane,
Watching, silent, from my window
People scurry in the rain.

Darkness falling, yet still early
Clouds of grey block out the light,
Watch the hands of time move slowly
Dragging on towards the night.

Streets fall silent, only patter
Of the rain outside remains,
Bleakness of the grey half-darkness
Chills the life inside my veins.

Wrapping up, against the coldness
Step out on the dull-grey street.
Misty drizzle casts half-shadows
Frozen pathways chill my feet.

Entering the busy high street
Floods of light fall on the road,
Glistening, gleaming in the wetness
Stands the stars of screen's abode.

Picture palace, realms of fancy,
Fantasy lives, Utopian dream,
Escape into the plush warm darkness,
Animated figures fill the screen.

Watch them dancing, singing, laughing,
From grim reality you will hide,
'Til the film draws to a close
And you are back on the grey outside.

Rebecca Summers

After the Film

After the film
i sit
in the car and
vaguely
hear fragments of
footsteps
but only see
the man
for a second.
i think
tenderness in
the showers
that rain on my
face is
too beautiful
to bear.
So, crying
film star tears
i, eyes closed and
seeing,
know the meaning
of soft silence.

Julie Williams

Chapter 10

Thank you, Mister Hitler!

Cinema at War

Bristol's cinemas suffered along with the rest of the city under Hitler's aerial onslaughts. The biggest loss was the Regent, on November 24th, 1940. Luckily, the cinema was closed that Sunday, but was due for its first Sunday opening a week later, when the Luftwaffe could well have caught the 2,000 seater with a full house.

There were other losses, including the Triangle, Clifton, a little past its prime yet still in good trim, and a few hundred yards away, the Coliseum, one-time skating rink and fashionable 1920's rendezvous was beyond repair. Others were damaged, including the popular New Palace but luckily only half a dozen cinemas were completely destroyed.

The Redcliffe picture house went, while a few yards away St. Mary Redcliffe Church miraculously escaped, and the Avonmouth and Stoll cinemas were other casualties. **Mr W. E. Davies** was in the audience that Good Friday night:

'Two friends and I went to the Stoll cinema in Bedminster to see **Tom Brown's Schooldays**. We could only afford the cheap seats in the front, so we had to look up at the screen. While we were watching the film, a bomb dropped on the cinema, the point of impact was just in front of the screen. It exploded, blasting the screen and wall behind into the street, which left us with a good view outside. Most of the people in the front seats were knocked

unconscious. As we were regaining consciousness, others from the back of the cinema were helping us to get up.

'The cinema manager said if we wanted to remain while the raid was still on, we could sit at the back, and they would play some music until the raid was over. We sat by the boards at the back, looking around and saw two girls who worked at the same factory as us. We were talking only a short time when the second bomb fell and exploded. The point of impact was at the top of the steps, outside the ticket office about ten feet away from us. The next thing I remember was being in a heap of people. I noticed one of the girls was trying to move, so I helped her to her feet. There was no dust in the air, so we must have been 'out' for some time. I looked up and saw a large hole in the roof; there was debris and glass everywhere. Then I made my way home to St Philips Marsh, with the air raid still raining down on the city.'

With the pounding that central Bristol endured those terrible nights, the New Palace [later, the Gaumont] incredibly lost less than three days working time during the whole war, even though Baldwin Street was regularly showered with bombs. Its war-time manager, **Mr G. H. Blackburn** was later to write:

'Soon after six o'clock, the alert sounded. The projection room being on the roof, it was advisable to discontinue the show and stow the highly flammable films in their fire-proof lockers.

'Some people left for home, or shelter, but 700 to 800 remained. Until the raid was over, well after midnight, the audience amused themselves with an impromptu concert, story telling etc, with bomb explosions taking the place of applause. The concert was more or less successful until a bomb dropped at the back of the building in Clare Street and a shower of debris fell through our roof a few inches behind where the singers were standing.

'... The concert dragged somewhat after this, but the salesgirl did a roaring trade with cigarettes and chocolate. Fires were raging all around, and sighs of relief were evident when at last the all clear was sounded.'

Attendances quickly recovered after the raids. Bomb craters, blocked streets and lengthy detours couldn't keep Bristolians from their favourite cinemas. As Charles Anderson commented in *A City and its Cinemas* (Redcliffe Press, out of print):

> The picture of the New Palace's patrons picking their way through a dangerously damaged city to get to the evening show has a quality that matches its times.

For **Mrs Pat James** 'as we grew older, going to the pictures became our only escape from the grim reality of the war, and the constant blitzes on the city. Hollywood offered everything lacking in our own lives: glamour, colour, beautifully dressed women. There were some wonderful stories. I always remember the Ziegfield Follies, and the Fred Astaire and Ginger Rogers films. One of my proudest boasts is that many years later I met Fred Astaire's daughter, who insisted I borrow a pair of her father's slip-on wellies to walk down a muddy lane. I almost floated down that path, trying out a few dance steps on the way.

'...In those days, you could enter halfway through a film and leave when you came to the part where you came in. People often stayed to catch the film over again.

'...As teenagers, we often tried to see 'A' films without an adult. These films could be considered totally innocent these days. Once, I agreed to take my brother and nephew to see one at the 'Maj', so wearing my sister's high heels and lipstick and feeling very grown up I queued with my giggling accomplices. The usher spotted me and when questioned, I admitted to being thirteen. I travelled home crushed, with the boys' scornful remarks accompanying me all the way.

'...I am still an ardent cinemagoer, and the films are better than ever. But something is missing.

The Odeon cinema

The atmosphere of the packed houses in the resplendent old cinemas added a sparkle to the evening's entertainment which the sterile boxes of today cannot supply.'

Mrs James recalls with horror the newsreels which showed the allied soldiers entering the Nazi concentration camps. 'It was terrible to realise that the images we shuddered at were only shadows of the real thing. Since then we have always protested strongly against any sign of fascism, for it must never be allowed to happen again.'

And speaking for most of the hundreds who wrote in, she concludes:

'Now in the age of television, sitting at home does not begin to compare with the thrill of being part of an audience, sitting together, expectantly, sharing the magic that only cinema can give.'

Mrs Patricia Edmead is another to recall that cinema wasn't all escapism.

'We learned the shocking truth about the holocaust and Belsen at the cinema. I don't think we could take it in. It was so awful and unlike the make believe world we all wanted to see. What a rude awakening.

'...But I will always be glad we had the escapism when we needed it. My interest started in the 1930s, with the opening of the Cabot Cinema in Filton. The main film was **The Good Ship Lollipop**, with Shirley Temple, and every child was given a free lollipop as they went in.

'The Odeon served tea on the balcony in the afternoons, and the New Palace had an organist who would rise up, playing, on to the stage during the interval. An unusual feature of the Eastville Hippodrome were the double seats for courting couples. The decor of thick carpets and velvet curtains lent luxury to the magic of sitting in the dark watching glamorous images and hearing the music.

'... In the forties, I was escorted to the King's Cinema by an American soldier to see **The Glenn Miller Story.** The accents of the GI servicemen and the scent of their cigars all added to the novelty and the pleasure of the films.

'The cinemas are not so glamorous now, and there is only one film. Still, there are some brilliant, well made films today, and I will always be a film fan.'

Mrs Doreen Mallitt was in the Odeon watching **The Mikado** when the film was stopped and the manager announced that an air raid was in progress.

'Anyone wishing to take cover should do so, but the film would continue for those who wished to stay. As a fearless fifteen-year-old I braved the peril.

'When the Americans took us into our picture houses they were amazed that people were allowed to smoke. It has been banned in their cinemas for a long time.

'Of course these darkened auditoriums had their share of perverts. In the Palace in Baldwin Street, a shocker ran his hand up my leg as he raised his seat, so, as he passed in front of me I punched him, with all my might, in the small of his back and he almost fell over into the row in front. The audience gasped, but he ran out of the exit like greased lightning!

'The war newsreels that reduced me to tears were numerous. The first that horrified me was of German soldiers abusing the Jews and burning their bibles. My Dad said, "You'll have to stop going if it upsets you so much."

'Ah, the memories come flooding back and all those reels of film have left indelible messages of life's rich pattern and the way to handle problems with dignity, instead of the senseless violence we see in our films so much today.'

Mr D. C Beard's first, unforgettable cinema experience was just after the war had ended.

'I was a young boy of seven and my mother, one dark evening, took me just up the road to Sussex Place to see all the lights on the front of the Metropole Cinema switched on again after the blackout of the war years.

'What a lovely sight. The blues, greens and yellows all shining out again. What a cheer went up from the crowd of people gathered there!'

Chapter 11

Extras 3

No place like home

John held his hand against the recognition panel and the door of his 24th floor Galleries apartment slid open. A green flashing light on the video phone indicated that there was a message waiting. He pressed the view button and Clare's face appeared.

'Hi,' she said, 'I'm at The Shed. Why don't you come down?'

Twenty minutes later he found her sitting in a quiet corner of the bar.

He bent down to kiss her on the cheek. 'Why'd you make me trek all the way over here?'

'Thought we might see a film,' she replied, glancing down her watch.

'Well, we could go back to my place.'

'I feel like a change of scenery.'

John sank into a chair. He remembered the last time they'd rented a cubicle and accessed one of the latest releases.

'Those hire helmets never seem to fit me,' he complained.

Clare leant forward. "I wasn't thinking of a cube. I've heard about a place, outside.'

John's eyes widened. "It's not safe at night. Is it?'

'It's perfectly safe. Trust me.'

John hesitated and then shrugged. "Okay.'

They left by the Augustine Exit and found themselves on a grey street. Climbing past the crumbling pillars of an old hall, they reached a deserted junction. Bearing right, the road led downhill.

'That used to be a hospital,' Clare said, taking John's hand.

He looked and thought he could make out a body, lying in the shadows. Away to the right, the towering walls of the Galleries were broken only by its bright, guarded entrances. John had rarely seen the complex from the outside and never after dark.

'Clare, where exactly are we going?'

'Almost there,' she answered, as they turned into a small square. The buildings were boarded up, although one doorway was lit. They stopped at a badly cracked, red sign. John read New Mayflower Chinese Restaurant, in faded yellow letters.

'I thought we were seeing a film,' he said, pulling his hand free.

'Trust me,' said Clare.

She stepped up to the door and knocked three times, waited a moment, then twice more. A small grill opened and a pair of eyes appeared. 'Table for two,' said Clare.

'In whose name is the reservation?' asked a voice.

'Oscar,' replied Clare, without hesitation.

The door opened and she led John in, her hand against the small of his back. They walked along a dimly lit corridor and came to another set of doors.

Clare pulled one open and steered John ahead of her. The room was dark and there was music playing. Fifty or more faces turned in their direction and John froze.

'Clare,' he hissed. 'This is illegal. The Assembly Laws don't allow...'

He was silenced by a loud 'Sssshhhh'. Clare stepped forward and folded down a seat. Reluctantly, John sat down.

As he looked up, a scene appeared on the screen. A young girl carrying a basket walked towards the gathering storm clouds with a small dog at her heels.

Lewis Ogle

Why not a British National Cinema?

Look at the British film charts in any week and you will see American films flooding the top-ten. This trend is largely accepted as, after all, America is one of the largest film producers and distributors, especially in the English speaking world. But what if we question this high number of imports? What has happened to the British film industry? An industry which, every few years, is announced to be making a comeback. Every time a British film does well in the British film charts, everyone is amazed, even more so when a British film hits number one in America! But, in the words of Barry Norman, 'Why not?'

In Britain today there are plenty of talented writers, directors and actors, yet very few independent, totally British (by that I mean produced and financed) films. There are of course a few notable exceptions, but most films are now made as co-productions with either the BBC or Channel 4. These films hardly ever receive a cinema release in any of the large cinema chains. Therefore, most British film productions rely on television for financial backing, or else are produced independently on low budgets.

This is not to blame American films for our failures. A more positive government policy towards film making, or the setting up of an independent financing system, might enable film makers to compete.

In America, film making is big business. It is a profit making concern which, although this limits the range of films made, at least gets the films produced. On the continent, film has always been seen as an art form and national cinema is viewed as an important aspect in creating national identity. Britain today seems to have fallen between these two approaches, with film largely seen as neither profitable nor art.

We go to the cinema and think nothing of the fact that most of the films showing are American. We watch Americans coping with their American problems, conflicts, adventures. But is this all relevant to us? How unusual to go to the cinema to see a British film, which shows British conflicts, problems, dramas. But why should it be unusual? Why should we not have a national cinema which reflects the diversity of British society and experiences more closely? There is more than enough material and talent to produce these films, yet we lack the finance, and until this problem is addressed, with either film making being seen as a profit making business or else funded as an art form, our cinemas will continue to be swamped by Americana.

Rebecca Summers

Moving pictures...

A glimpse of my mum (told to me) as I wish I'd known her - a carefree girl eating marmalade sandwiches in the interval between the two parts of **Gone with the wind**. Twelve years on she would have two children and be cruelly paralysed by multiple sclerosis. To my dad, then, fell the task of appearing carefree for us and taking my brother and me to the cinema for Saturday treats. Our excitement was his.

'Are you enjoying yourself?' he whispered as I

feasted my eyes on **The Conquest of Everest**. I remember how he pressed my hand when I nodded with happiness.

In my teens, sullen and lost, slipping from school through the caretaker's gate to escape VI form science and pass the time with Rita Tushingham and **The Leather Boys**.

Not so long after, a probationer teacher taking my own class of leather boys to **Henry V** and constantly assuring them that the battle scenes were worth waiting for.

A mother myself and first in the queue for **Star Wars** and **Superman** (I like to believe a man can fly) with a bag of sandwiches for two. Temporary heroine to my young son asking him if he is enjoying himself, pressing his hand with excited solidarity.

Later, an evening in an empty cinema (Henleaze held a golden oldies night - few came) and a showing of **Yankee Doodle Dandy** just for my husband and me. I felt like a queen.

To echo George Cohen as James Cagney echoes him in that film of films - creators of cinema - my mother thanks you, my father thanks you, my son thanks you, my husband thanks you. And I thank you.

Geraldine Taylor

Sam Rewrites Casablanca

'Forget Paris, Rick' I said
'And forget that song.
You'll only start getting moody,
sink seven or eight bourbons,
then do your stupid impression of Hitler
invading Poland. It worries the clientele.
It isn't funny
when you finally fall off your chair, singing
the unofficial version of
'Deutschland Uber Alles'
and end up with your face on somebody's files.

'The girl's no good, I'm telling you.
I heard she had an affair
with Mussolini. Or maybe it was Rossellini.
Don't look at me like that.
If you had any sense about anything
you wouldn't be wearing a white tuxedo.
It shows the dirt
and this is a dirty town.
And as for women... Listen,
you're not the first to be charmed
by her taste in hats
and Scandinavian accent.

'You hear me?
Forget Paris, Rick
and forget that song.
Find someone younger.
Someone who knows how to whistle.'

Tony Lewis - Jones

First Date

He was late.
The air was laced with ice and chattering crowds
She noticed how girls met loves with easy smiles
And linking arms followed a thinning line into warmth and light.

Moving back against peeling posters
She willed him to come after hours of effort
Polishing nails, pressing clothes, preparing words.

There were running footsteps as the doorman cast her a last kind smile.
He kicked through rolling papers pale as slivers of moon
His arms flapping into a milky white coat
Like a bedraggled seagull black eyes peering for her.

He caught her hand, apologising about work and buses
And they slipped last into a dark flickering heat.

Images flowed silently - an excuse for their presence
Around couples kissed, murmured and she envied their confident laughter.

But this was their first date
And she trembled when he gently braceleted her wrist
His hand slowly tracing the shape of hers.

Amidst this drift of smoke and sound and light
A public romance and a private haze of bliss.

Sam Nixon

Cinders at the Cinema

She talked to the wall
that's the bit
that sticks in my mind
the night at the cinema
when we watched
Shirley Valentine.

Her zest for living
lost,
along with her plans
somewhere between Sainsburys
and the frying pan.

And we three watched
a little smug
snug in our velour seats
with our packet of 'poppets'
and boiled sweets.

'Most of us are dead'
she said
'long before we die'
she told her kitchen wall
but she got no reply.

There was a rustle
in the audience
as we all stirred
it peeled at our wrappings
and left us unnerved.

For there in the mirror
with the world
up for grabs
was a middle-aged housewife
with carrier bags.

Surplus to requirements
she unhooked
and took the plunge
then flew off to Mykonas
an island in the sun.

The journey of her dreams
she had made her life change
no longer Shirley
in compartments
she had found herself again.
And then it was over
but in the dark
just a tiny spark
was left behind
the night at the cinema
when we watched
Shirley Valentine.

Christine Curry

Chapter 12

Extras 4

Designer cinema

To most people the idea of being involved in the making of a film probably seems the epitome of glamour. Of course it's not really, especially since the old star system died a death. There are some actors who still insist on the chauffeur-driven limousine and an entire floor of a hotel to themselves, but they are not appreciated as it eats up someone else's chunk of the budget. Most people involved in a film simply roll up their sleeves and get on with it, driven by their love of the business to work sixteen hours a day often in difficult conditions.

I worked as a costume designer for fifteen years and saw many well known figures in their undies, bringing home the fact that we are all the same under the Jean-Paul Gautier labels. The costume department is a great leveller, where insecurities are brought to the surface like bubbles in the bath, and where the soothing oil of flattery has to be poured over the troubled waters of vanity for a quiet life. Where you realise that no man can be trusted to tell you the correct size of his jock strap, and no woman the current circumference of her waist. That the handsome Lothario suffers from halitosis, and the femme fatale is paranoid about the size of her bust. As one actress said regretfully as she posed sideways in front of the mirror, 'There's the bosom that launched a thousand dinghies'.

If a film star continues to be a pain in the butt, a plot is usually devised to get even. When Sophia Loren was working on a film set in England and was giving the crew a seriously hard time, the 'sparks' concealed a microphone in the bathroom of her private caravan and connected it to the tannoi system. She never knew that every time she used it, intimate noises were relayed at full volume to everyone present.

There is fun but precious little glamour in the job. As a costume designer you develop ape-like arms from carrying twenty bags of clothes, shoes and lengths of cloth round the West End on a shopping expedition. (You'll never know how heavy six pairs of shoes can be until you try it.) Not to mention a cast iron sphincter, since it is impossible to get yourself and the bags into a loo, and equally impossible to leave the bags outside. You are likely to spend all your winters dressed as a hot water cylinder in quilted orange nylon standing in a freezing field with wellington boots taking root in the mud, and all your summers in a dark and airless studio seeing no daylight for months.

And yet, because of the way filming absorbs your life, the crew for the duration becomes your family, for whom you would move mountains and vice versa. Once on my birthday, cold and tired at the end of the day, they triumphantly produced for me out of the middle of the Yorkshire moors, a plastic bag containing a bottle of champagne surrounded by ice cubes. I don't even like champagne, but it warmed me none-the-less.

It's a wonderfully awful business.

Kate Fox

Con-artists of the cine-camera

I have seen more than 10,000 of the films listed in Halliwell's Film Guide, some several times, but one film typifies the hypnotic effect of the film camera, an hypnosis that has affected me on hundreds of occasions.

For many people, a film based on a novel or stage play very rarely equals the quality or impact of the written original. How much more rare, therefore for a film to TRANSCEND the quality of its written source. The reason has to be something inherent in the Art of Film itself, and that typically means camerawork of genius.

Many years ago, a friend asked me to accompany him to a cinema with four choices of film, and I assumed without asking which film we would see. It was not until titles began to roll that I realised that the film was **Siddhartha**, based on a novel by Hermann Hesse, one of the many modern novelists whose works I deeply dislike. Only common courtesy prevented my walking out of the cinema.

Then the film began, and I became unaware of the building, the people, the screen, totally unaware of anything but the flowing pictorial presentation. I only vaguely followed the story but was spellbound by sights and scenes of India, as photographed by Sven Nykvist, Ingmar Bergman's special cinematographer. I was transported by the sequence of images and colours poured into my eyes and up my nerve threads to the brain.

When the film finished, shimmering with rich colour to the last, I sat for several minutes before seeking the outside world, and the busy streets of the car journey. I still dislike the novels of Hermann Hesse but I am in no doubt about the hypnotic power of the movie camera in the hands of a genius.

This experience caused me to reflect on my hundred favourite films, and I found that, although over half are in black and white film, they depend very largely on seductive use of the camera, which is proper to an art form founded and fashioned on the intensified images of great cinematographers.

Bill Pickard

A hill of beans

Rick's Café, Casablanca. Say it to yourself. It still doesn't ring true after all this time. Rick's Café, Chicago maybe. Or Rick's Cafe, Perry, Oklahoma. But Casablanca? What's this guy doing stuck in a flyblown outpost of Nazi controlled Vichy France? (Apart, that is, from looking cool in a white jacket, and playing the suave host.) He says he came for the waters. But he's such an ironist you're never sure when he's wisecracking. Captain Renault isn't: 'What waters? We're in the desert.' 'I was misinformed,' says Rick. And we know we're not going to find out how he got here.

Rick Blaine. Café proprietor. Someone who stays out of trouble. Who doesn't take sides. 'I stick out my neck for nobody. I'm the only cause I'm interested in.' But this show of world-weary disinterest doesn't convince. We know he has a past. If, like Gatsby, it's a slightly shady one gun-running Ethiopia - at least we know he's prepared to muck in. He won't stay neutral forever.

Sure enough, he cracks. And it didn't really take very much, did it? A young couple, very much in love, need visas badly, only they're short of readies. Rick gives the croupier the nod and suddenly they start winning at roulette. Perhaps love is Rick's only criteria for action, perhaps it is only affairs of the heart which dictate his moral choices. But the nagging doubt is there: what might he do when this crazy business between these Europeans crashes in on him?

When Ilse Lund shows up with Victor Laszlo, we seem to get our answer. Rick and Ilse rekindle their flame while resistance hero Victor plays cat and mouse with Major Strasser. Rick can't say out of this one. The roulette couple were, after all, Rick and Ilse in another time and another place. In Paris, they didn' t make it out together. This time it'll be different. Rick'll see to that. He's thinking for both of them.

A surprise. then, at the denouement. 'You're getting on that plane with Victor Laszlo,' Rick tells Ilse. Ilse's eyes well up with tears, and we recognise that something more than the dynamics of love is at play. Brandishing his pistol, giving orders, this is the old Rick, the gun-running Rick. Ilse may be Rick 's green light at the end of the dock, but, unlike Gatsby, he's not trying to beat against the current. He rides it, and lets the green light fade out as the plane soars off towards Lisbon. Rick, we understand, has signed up to someone else's cause.

So this is Rick Blaine, a man prepared to commit. Rick of Casablanca. Casablanca: the White House. Rick, the American, the former neutral, eschews isolationism and chooses hope over fear, struggle over surrender, defiance over complicity. This is 1942. This is America joining the war.

Adrian Paul

I wanted to be a star

Biko was filmed in Zimbabwe - the nearest (and perhaps cheapest) equivalent to the forbidden territory of South Africa. My friend Claude was heavily involved. An assistant director, he got time off from his regular accountant job, and earned some amazing sums of money for a Zimbabwean - all those American notes make a lot of bucks when you change them into Zim dollars. It was a glamorous job, involving long trips off into the wilderness with crates of beer and plenty of parties. I couldn't go, it being in the school term, and only saw him sporadically, in between long shoots. One day, he came home treading the clouds. He was going to be in **Biko**, as well as of it. The third football player or was it the fourth? Three days filming - and extra money. Then they gave him a speaking part. Three words, and even more money.

Money was what it was all about really. Now at last the chance to leap beyond your greatest aspirations - hiring, firing, dining, wining (lots of that). It was wild! And every one dreamed of getting in with the movie crowd. But it wasn't easy. The foreign film companies preferred to import even down to the kitchen sink in some cases. And if they did employ locally you could bet your bottom dollar (as long as it's not American) that they weren't as well paid.

King Solomon's Mines caused a bit of a stink. Reports came through that white extras were paid more than black ones. Why oh why? raged the papers. Black actors were two a penny and whites were difficult to find came the reply. Still, I wouldn't like to knock **King Solomon's Mines** too much. One of my students owed her 'O' Levels to that film. She had lost her fees on the way to the classroom, fainting in the sun. And when she recovered the money was gone. No chance of getting any more in that poverty-stricken township and she was one of the brightest girls. I spent a horrible time collecting from scoffing staff. 'Lost it?' 'More likely spent it.' But as I pointed out she was the Head Girl and if we couldn't trust her, then well who could we trust? It was a good argument. It got her forty dollars. And you guessed it, she made up the extra as an extra in **King Solomon's Mines** though I never never saw her in the film.

Back to **Biko**, and the première - a big night. Hugh Masekela was performing with his trumpet. I'd got dressed up for it - and we were very nearly late, the car having run out of petrol. Don't know where all those extra bucks had gone. Still we were in time to see Claude, and he had warned me not to blink - three words don't last long. We saved our bated breath for the credits, looking out for the directorial contribution. Not a sign, not a smidgen - he wasn't there at all. Just a three second bit part. 'Though you did fill the screen for that,' I said.

'I would rather not have been in it at all. It means nothing at all. It means nothing: third football player - I wanted to be a star.'

Judy Kendall

Chapter 13

Yes, those were the Good Old Days

Good evening, madam

I was born and brought up in Triangle West, where my mother had a fruit and flower shop opposite the Triangle Cinema. I do not know when it was built but to me and my sister, it was always there.

It was owned by Mr Harris, who was very popular and well respected in the neighbourhood. It was in those days quite a large and very comfortable cinema, with plenty of room to stretch your legs, people could get to their seats without your having to get up.

There was of course a balcony where the usherettes would serve afternoon tea during the interval. We had a relative who played the piano; she would see a run through of the programme and had to decide what to play during the showing.

The films were changed on Thursday. There was the feature, or main film, a shorter one, then a cartoon, I remember Felix the Cat, and a newsreel. Of course, it was all silent films at that time and we saw Charlie Chaplin, Buster Keaton and Harold Lloyd and of course actresses like Pearl White.

Many of the stars of those days were finished because their voices did not record well when the talking films started.

The first talking one I saw was I believe called **The Hebe** with an actor called Reg Toomey. Then came Al Jolson with **The Jazz Singer** which everybody thought was wonderful, and the **Broadway Melody** film.

I remember seeing Marie Dressler and Wallace Beery in **Tug Boat Annie**. I may be wrong, but I have a feeling that Greta Garbo was in it, her first film; and of course **The Blue Angel** with Marlene Dietrich. It was all so much glamour in our young lives.

Mr Harris was always in the vestibule to greet the customers in lounge suit in the afternoons, and dinner jacket at night. He always spoke to people and thanked them for coming. It was almost like a family cinema, people would go every week, and when the lights went up you would know so many people, and of course the usherettes got to know people quite well.

In those days before the war, if a boy asked a girl to go out, it was always to the pictures. Girls did not go into public houses in those days, so it was the films or a walk.

On Saturday nights, there was usually a queue, and a man would come with a barrel organ, to entertain the crowd. They were often wet and cold, but it did not worry them, as they knew they would be warm when they were inside.

When the Regent Cinema opened up in Castle Street, we thought that maybe customers would leave the Triangle, but they didn't. To the local people, the Regent wasn't the same, somehow. But all that ended on the first night of the blitz, when we saw our own very loved cinema burnt to the ground. It was like losing a very dear friend. I am eighty years old now, but I always remember the happy hours I spent in the Triangle.

Kay Rice-Hawker

The Triangle cinema

His Majesty's displeasure

During World War Two, **Mrs Dora Haile** owned a ladies' hairdressing business in Fishponds.

'As permanent waving solution was difficult to obtain I endeavoured to make my own if I could get the necessary ingredients, including 880 ammonia which was very strong.

'On my day off, I decided with my sister-in-law to go to His Majesty's Cinema in Eastville. Next to the cinema was a chemist shop, and the chemist filled a medicine bottle with the solution for me. Very pleased with myself, off I went into the cinema. Half way through the film, the cinema was filled with ammonia fumes, and everyone was coughing and spluttering. The heat in the cinema had raised the cork.

'Usherettes sprayed perfume around, and all I could do was quietly keep my foot on the cork. In the interval, we crept out with red faces, although I must say it was all very realistic, as a film about scientists was being shown at the time.'

Fay Cooper remembers:

'When we entertained friends at home, the conversation often turned to silent film, and I heard long accounts of the doings of Charlie Chaplin, Mary Pickford, Valentino and many more.

'My initiation into 'the pictures' was to see a showing of Disney 'shorts' when I was three. Our nearest cinema was the Carlton. The Piccadilly, Waldorf and Olympia were all within easy reach, and the Rialto and Robin Hood only a short bus ride away. These were respectable houses, except for the Olympia, which my mother called a 'flea pit', though neither of us ever caught a flea there.

'...I was impressed by the glitzy modern interiors depicted on screen, but not by the costumes, which I often thought unbecoming. Those women stars, though, I doted on and longed to be one of them. When I see them on television now, I still think they were great.

For me, no other industrial product can equal the glamour of those Hollywood films. They were so streamlined, including the actors. Only the other day, I watched on television a 1930's hospital film, called **Four Women in White**. It charted the progress of four student nurses to qualification. They were so artificially slender and so completely standardised it was difficult to tell them apart.

'...Whatever the stereotyping, I regretted the passing of the great days of Hollywood, and by 1950 felt I had had the best of the cinema. I gave it up, except for an occasional Russian or Japanese film, and visits to a film society, where I caught up with the silent films I had missed.

The big attraction at Filton's Cabot cinema in October, 1935. The Cabot seated 1,114 and prices ranged from 6d in the front stalls to 1/3d for the best seats in the circle.

In the 1930s **Stanley Waits** was a regular cinema goer. 'The Premier on Gloucester Road, Horfield was my main haunt, but I also went to the Scala, the Plaza and in the winter to Bristol North Baths, which were covered over and chairs set out for seats unlike the tip ups in the regular cinemas.

'Both the Scala and the Plaza put on live variety at times with acts between the films. Being still at school, for an 'A' Certificate I had to give my money to an adult and go in with them. Could you imagine that happening in today's society?

'When I was older, the Regent was an outstanding cinema, with Colin Howson on the organ. They had occasional stage shows. One was Film Star Something and another, Caroll Lewis looking for talent before he toured the major variety theatres with his 'Discoveries'.

'One point of interest. The Hippodrome had converted to a cinema and just before it closed, Billie Houston made a personal appearance to present a cheque for a competition winner. She had been with her sister Renée in a top variety act as the Houston Sisters. When the Hippodrome reopened as a variety theatre, Renée topped the bill during the opening week.

'It's a great shame that these have gone. The Premier, a supermarket, The Scala and Regent gone completely and the Plaza [later the Academy] now a Christadelphia Chapel.'

From **Mrs Jean Woelfer**, ex-usherette at the Park Cinema in St George:

'... One thing that stands out in my memory was an old vagrant lady who sold Old Moore's Almanack. Once a week, always on a Thursday, she would come to the cinema, only during the winter months when the weather got colder. During the summer months she slept in St George's Park, and in the winter, in shop doorways. On her visits to the cinema, she wore several layers of clothes. Always paid in pennies and half-pennies. Then she would proceed to the front of the cinema, go to the end of the row next to the radiator and fall asleep. We always had to wake her at the end of the performance. I remember we always tried to keep that seat free for her on Thursdays.'

Memories flooded back, too, for **Mrs M. Little** ... of **The Wizard of Oz** being especially wonderful because she thought it was going to be in black and white....Of Saturday mornings at the ABC Whiteladies, where the kids were exhorted to ' sing aloud with glee, and all be pals together' ... school trips to the Embassy to see **Richard III** and a film of the Queen's coronation ... of gobstoppers at the Cabot which seemed a lot bigger than they are today...avidly reading the *Film-goer* every week...of dressing up with a friend as schoolgirls to get into the Odeon because they couldn't afford the adult ticket... walking miles to see a Mario Lanza film or any other musical at the Odeon Bedminster, Cabot at Filton or the Orpheus at Henleaze, besides at least the ten within easy walking of Kingsdown, where she grew up...but above all, of meeting her future husband at the King's in 1959, during a showing of **Tom Thumb**.

A showman's heyday

1933 from an employment standpoint was as difficult as today. I had finished full time education and had every intention of seeking a job as a science teacher! I heard that the local silent cinema was to re-open with sound so I contacted the proprietor and was engaged as assistant projectionist. The pay was appalling - but it was a job and my long standing interest in matters electric and photographic, radio and sound amplification stood me in good stead. Within six months I had assimilated enough skill in cinema technique to take over the running of the cinema show.

In 1940 I came to Bristol and joined a small privately owned cinema group as a chief projectionist. I remained with the firm until I retired 38 years later - with few regrets. I worked first as projectionist and then as a manager - and what changes we saw during that time and since.

The projectionist had to be a 'showman'. Coloured lighting and sound control had to be operated with constant attention to the screen illumination. This was by high powered carbon arcs operating at some 2,000°c and the intensity of light provided in skilled hands has never been bettered even today. The lamps were hand fed at first and even when subsequently motorised they still needed continual attention. The film itself came in approx' 1000 foot reels, two of which were joined in sequence to give a running time of 22 mins. As one spool ran out a slick change of sound and picture to a second machine left the audience unaware that the change had been made - and this is where the showmanship skill came in.

The film at this time was cellulose nitrate - highly inflammable and dangerous. Chemically it was related to T.N.T. Safety regulations were very strict and in Bristol monitored regularly by Police and Fire Officers. Buckets of water and sand and an asbestos blanket had to be kept ready in event of trouble. It was a great relief when 'non-flam' acetate film became the norm as it meant that quite a few stringent regulations could be relaxed.

These days were the 'heydays' of the cinema and rightly so. Where today are the Great Musicals? The **King of Jazz** with its early colour sequences gave a glimpse of things to come culminating in what I consider to be the greatest of them all - **The Sound of Music.** After 100 viewings I knew every word and every note and yet I still enjoy it when it comes to T.V. **Oklahoma**, **Annie get your gun**, **Seven Brides** and dozens of others provided the audiences with real ENTERTAINMENT.

Eric King

A star is born

The cinema in Hassocks, at the foot of the South Downs, looked like the furniture repository it would probably become.

Most weeks, if you arrived after the doors opened for the afternoon performance there wasn't a queue. If you were early, or the management late, a small, rather lethargic group would huddle at the top of the steps under the somewhat incongruous canopy and look out on to the invariably empty car-park waiting for the manager to arrive in his ancient banger. To the ten year-old I then was, the space seemed enormous, and if there were more than two cars not only was it crowded, there were strangers in town.

But all this changed the week they screened **Once a Jolly Swagman** with Dirk Bogarde in his first starring role: for Dirk Bogarde was a local boy, and he was making good - very good as the passing years and a knighthood were to confirm.

Everybody knew him, at least by proxy - my mother met his nearly every week at the cheese counter of Hoadley's in Burgess Hill, the next village up the line, where we lived. Because everyone knew him we wanted to support him, share in the first fruits of his success and in some small way, feel that a little bit of 'celebrity' was rubbing off on us.

As usual my mother and I arrived just after the doors had opened and we looked round the deserted car-park in disbelief. The straggle of people encircling the gravelled patch was coming to some sort of order, ready to file towards the box office, small change already clutched in sticky hands.

The end of the queue overflowed on to the main road trailing back towards the railway station. We tagged on the back, hardly daring to hope that we would get in.

Somehow the building managed to swallow up all the waiting fans. What if we were too near the front and had to crane our necks to see the distorted images telling us of 'Coming Attractions' and the elongated cockerel crowing about last week's news, we were there, waiting impatiently as the lights went down after the supporting film, and the travelogue about some corner of the world which, in those days, might just as well have been part of another planet. Finally the curtains glowed pink and after a breathless moment began to part as they faded to black and the censor's certificate came up, its edges crumpled on the drapes.

Then the treasured name, the reflected glory and the beginning of a sort of love affair....

Ann Das

Sometimes on a Sunday

In the Sixties **Geraldine Maher** and her twin sister used to go the the lovely old Ritz Cinema in Brislington, sometimes twice a week. 'The hit of the day, **Becket** was showing and was due to finish its run on a Sunday. By Saturday we had been unable to get in, and despite strong parental disapproval, and some qualms on our part about going to the pictures on a Sunday, my sister and I went to the afternoon show. It was summer, and very hot both inside and outside on that day, and our discomfort was added to by the drama of the film. The moment when Richard Burton as Becket is struck down by the conspirators was approaching and the whole audience was on tenterhooks.

'The first dagger was raised... and at that moment there was an enormous clap of thunder outside as a storm raged overhead. My sister and I clutched at each other, quite convinced that it was the wrath of God on us for going to the cinema on a Sunday. We raced home in the pouring rain, absolutely sure that our parents would have something to say, but all we got was a knowing look, and a hot cup of tea with an admonition to "go and get dry now girls."

'It was a sad day when that lovely old cinema was closed.'

Lurch-baiting

My abiding cinema memories are of a man called Lurch. At least, that was his nickname. Tall, skinny, owlish glasses, acne and a grubby white coat straight out of Frankenstein's lab. He didn't own our local cinema but he ran it, taking the tickets, selling ice cream, ushering people to their seats and probably sweeping up when we had all gone home. In my youth he was Mr Cinema himself, and I can never go and see a film today without thinking of him, however fleetingly.

In our eyes any entertainment provided by the film itself was secondary compared to Lurch-baiting. The idea was to disrupt the running of the film as much as possible without getting physically thrown out of the cinema.

The first tactic we would use was to hook our feet over the row in front and start a rhythm going. This enabled you to test the water; would his torch snap on at the first thud of boot on cinema seat, or would he wait until you and your friends had carefully built it into a deafening crescendo of sound? The real trick was to anticipate him; to get your feet down and a look of innocence and studied interest in the film on your face in the second before the torch was shone in your direction.

The next stage involved moving around the cinema. Lurch was a fair man; he would always warn you first before he threw you out. So once you had the warning the trick was to disappear from that seat and emerge somewhere else. This confused him, and also gave you a chance to annoy any girls of your acquaintance as you moved from row to row. A master of this technique could cause such unrest that Lurch would throw the girls out.

We would then move to the crowning moment of the evening; improvising dialogue along with the sound track. Some gems I remember:

'He'll 'ave someone's eye out with that if he's not careful! ' During the gladiators scene in **Spartacus**.

'It's Auntie Doris!' During a three in a bed sex scene in **Stardust**.

'I'll get you back for that you rotter!'After the climactic shoot out in **The Wild Bunch**.

It was all in the timing, and if you could get the whole cinema laughing it was worth getting thrown out for. After all, it just meant finding an ingenious way of sneaking in again tomorrow to see the rest of it.

Oh Lurch, where are you now in these days of faceless multiplexes? The cinema where you worked is long gone, and I am writing this to thank you for giving me more excitement, fun and laughter than the films ever did.

J. M. Voake

Stoned in the back row

It must have been the late 1950s. As two new students at Newton Park College we'd had the extraordinary good luck to meet two flying chappies from South Cerney. One had a TR2! There wasn't much entertainment in those days so a visit to the Little Theatre, in Bath, to see a film, was as inevitable as was hanky-panky in the back row. The warm Indian summer evening was almost as close as we got, and the 'Carrying On' on the screen was rivalled only by that in the darker regions of the cinema...

The film was 'laugh a minute' stuff - all bosoms, bottoms and innuendo. The man to the left of me was a stranger with a brown paper bag. A bag full of ripe Victoria plums. Every now and then, at a moment thoughtfully chosen to coincide with gales of laughter from the punters, there would be a rustle of paper followed by a slurping sound which indicated that yet another Victoria plum had bitten the dust. Surprisingly, the man left before the end of the film. I untwined myself from the arms of my pilot, stretched, put my hand on to my lap and felt something hard, cold and wet. I leapt up and screamed. People 'shushed' and told me to 'sit down and shut up'.

Eventually a torch-flashing usherette arrived accompanied by the manager and I had to explain how I'd discovered that the man with the brown paper bag had been surreptitiously depositing sucked clean plum stones in my lap. 'You must have known' said the manager, but I hadn't, and the experience still rates as worse than any horror film I've ever seen.

Sue Stops

Smoke got in my eyes

My first movie memories were in the early 1950s, when I was allowed to go to the Ritz Cinema in Brislington Village on a Saturday morning. It was a wonderful treat, as we did not own a TV until 1960.

You can imagine how grown up I felt. We had to walk down the Rocks, just before Victoria

Park, way before it was all built on. When I was a little older, as we walked home from an evening showing, we would have to walk up this hill and if we had seen a creepy film, we couldn't get home quickly enough.

When I was first allowed to go to a grown up film, I think it was **The Dambusters**, my friend and I brought a packet of five Woodbines. I always looked older than I was, so although we were about 14 or 15, there was no problem getting them. Neither of us had smoked before, and just wanted to act grown up and impress some boys we thought would be there. We sat near the back, and as soon as the lights went down, out came the Woodbines and matches. We both lit up, spluttered, then sat with the cigarette in hand, letting the boys see our smoke rising. Neither of us took another puff, and have never smoked since.

But that incident remains etched on my memory: my first and last cigarette in the Ritz Cinema I was so sorry to see pulled down. And yes, I did also have a cuddle in the back row, but that is altogether another story!

Margaret Trigg

'Summer nights '

It was the summer of '78. All the girls desperately wanted to be Olivia Newton-John and all the boys fancied themselves as John Travolta! One question dominated conversations in the school playground - "How many times have you seen IT?"

'It' was of course **Grease**! 'Grease-Fever' swept through our school so relentlessly that teachers gave in under pressure and cancelled school trips to the zoo and seaside and took us to the pictures instead! But we were there again on Saturday - nearly every Saturday in fact ... for the whole summer!

The queue would wrap itself around the ABC cinema building, leaving in its wake a trail of empty crisp packets and sweet wrappers after the opening of the doors at precisely 1p.m. (not a second before) allowed us to heave and hurl ourselves inside to get the best seats! The previously restrained polite British queue gave way to hundreds of lethal 12 year olds prepared to kill, maim or dismember anyone who tried to hold them back. Ushers were flattened in the tidal wave and quickly gave up trying to check whether we had bought tickets or not!

Armed again with loud crisps, fizzy cans of coke and sweets wrapped in the world's noisiest wrappers, we impatiently sat through the short film and laughed at the local adverts. Then suddenly silence engulfed the cinema as **Grease** finally began. We knew the script inside out and backwards - we all had the photo-story film books! We knew all the words to the songs and yelled out the words when the time came! All the boys 'singing' the boys' parts and the girls 'singing' theirs!

Nearly two hours later we emerged... declaring it was the best film ever! Nothing could top it. Even those who had seen it 'at least 20 times' (so they said). After we'd all gone back home for tea, we'd go up to our rooms, get out the photo-story books, put on the record and relive the whole thing over again... each of us hoping deep down that the fantasy that was **Grease** would sometime happen to us.

Theresa Hardeley

Sorry and thanks

This is an apology and a thank you to the manager of the Arts Centre cinema, King Square.

I'm sorry me and my mate ripped you off. We knew that the admission price didn't cover both films. As we waited in our seats after **High Heels**, for **The Commitments** we hoped you wouldn't see us. You did. I can't remember exactly what you said but I know we played dumb, 'You mean that isn't for both films?' I think you knew but you smiled and said, 'Well, since you didn't know I'll let you off...' And we smiled back, nodding like idiots saying, 'Thanks, thanks.'

I don't know what my first film at The Arts Centre was, but I do remember doing a double take as I saw your sign underneath the larger one for the Chinese restaurant. Wandering along that dank corridor past the kitchens, I thought, 'Jesus, what a dump.' Then, as I sat down and looked around, I realised we were all just there for the film. It felt like somehow I belonged.

It's not a posey 'art house', like The Arnolfini or The Watershed or a multiscreened, pop corn crunching, piece of America. It's just there to show good films. I don't talk to the others in the audience (sometimes there aren't many of us) but I know they feel the same way. They come to see the films in a cinema, not a very big one, but a cinema. Often you're their last chance before they're consigned to video.

Admit it, you let us off, didn't you? You let us off because you love films and it pleased you that we'd gone that far to watch one. So sorry for ripping you off and thanks for letting us stay. Thanks for everything else.

Lee Bryant

The staff at the Empire cinema (1936 - 37)

The striking modernist lines of the Ambassador cinema which opened in Kingswood in March 1938. The programme included British Movietone News, a Mickey Mouse cartoon and Jessie Matthews in *Sailing Along*.

Chapter 14

Who really dunnit?

John Winstone

The 1955 centenary of the birth of William Friese-Greene resurrected him as pioneer and possibly inventor of cinematography. The associated publicity produced a counter claim from the American camp. Despite widespread acceptance of the latter view the true picture has remained muddied by lack of proper research.

It was Mrs Emily Richardson's little tabby that wandered between the Lord Mayor's and Reece Winstone's legs, down the steps of 12 College Street, played with the mike leads and pretty much stole the unveiling ceremony of a plaque to mark the centenary of the birth of the Bristol-born pioneer of cinematography in 1955. The police constable marshalling sixty of Bristol's great, good and curious, gathered with such effort by Reece, was in his shirt sleeves in the late afternoon September sun - his sergeant opening the Lord Mayor's car door kept his tunic on. The writer, schoolboy-blazered, dad's camera in hand, was only half aware of the poignant contrast between the quiet decrepitude of Georgian College Street and the new white Portland stone of the rear of Bristol's Council House that rose up facing it. College Street and generous fronted No 12, 5 bays of patchy raddle washed stucco (a colour once commonplace in Bristol), even then were marked for demolition, as Reece reminded them in his opening remarks and made his plea for retention.

The screening of **The Magic Box**, John Boulting's contribution to the Festival of Britain, had alerted Reece to Friese-Greene as an unsung Bristolian; as he wrote, 'In January 1952, I came out of my local cinema with some mixed but very deep emotions.' It was Ray Allister, *nom de plume* of Mrs Muriel Forth, whose biography, *Friese-Greene Close up of an Inventor*, first saw in him the romance of the inventor. She recounted to Reece, when he had tracked her down, how Boulting's secretary had put her book in his hands when rained off a film set, how she was telegrammed to join him and, there and then, an option was taken for a film. Reece, a keen cinema goer and admirer of Allister, was much younger than her, only forty-seven in 1955 and still two years from commencing his own series of books, but blessed with the retrospection that can accompany middle age. He explained in a radio broadcast in 1955 how he had 'long sympathized with courageous spirits who had tried, in the past, to obtain some suitable memorial in the city of his birth. In the period betweeen the wars, several citizens took up the campaign but all to no avail.' These included G.H. Blackburn, present at the meeting where Friese-Greene collapsed and died, Mr G. Pugsley, proprietor of the Orpheus cinema, R. F. Warne, photographic dealer; A. Pereira FRPS, at the 1948 Royal Photographic Society Bristol Conference; even Alistair Cooke, broadcasting in 1930. 'Suddenly a flash of inspiration came: 1855-1955; *the centenary of the birth of Friese-Greene.* Surely such an event could be the time to make another plea for recognition.' At this time he had no idea of the location of the birthplace.

The BBC declined to re-broadcast **The Magic Box** for the centenary. Settling on a plaque came as second nature to Reece; he had developed a foresight for anticipating anniversaries to gain publication of unsolicited, illustrated articles in periodicals. In addition, London had led the way in March the previous year with a plaque to the 'Pioneer of Cinematography' at Friese-Greene's 1888-91 home, 136 Maida Vale. Reece asked that they do more, but the Corporation of London declined, partly because the necessary consent of the owner of 92 Piccadilly (his business address at the time of the 1889 patent) had not been forthcoming. And there were also parallels for Reece. 'I even feel a strange affinity with

William Friese-Greene

Friese-Greene - I too was born, educated, married and entered professional photography in Bristol; I have enjoyed membership of the Bath P.S., R.P.S. and R.S.A., the same as he.' The family, Friese-Greene's surviving sons by his second wife, Graham, Kenneth and Maurice, grandsons Peter, Anthony and John, nephew Tony and Friese-Greene's cousin T. C. Leaman of Bath, were of course most gratified by Reece's efforts. They eagerly corresponded, Graham in particular who had contributed various papers on his father's work and was an artist in metals. He designed and his company, J Starkie Gardner Ltd, manufactured the green-patinated bronze plaque for No 12, as well as a wall tablet set up in St George's, Brandon Hill, the following month.

The centenary programme occupied a full day starting with Reece's first experience of radio at 8.15 am, when his outpourings were heard in Derby by Mrs Ethel Barnes, Friese-Greene's first child who was to die the following year. Reece's old friend, P. G.Field, president of the Western Counties Photographic Federation, was collected at Temple Meads in 'that wonderful electric-blue car' (Allister's description of Reece Winstone's MkVII Jaguar). Thence to 67 Queen's Road for the re-unveiling of an existing plaque to a one-time studio before a celebration lunch courtesy of the Queen's Road Association at the Berkeley. A quick visit to the City Museum and Art Gallery to look at Reece's photo-biography display, before dropping into St George's, the school church for Queen Elizabeth's Hospital where Friese-Greene was a pupil (and where Mr Green extended his name to Friese and added the 'e' to Green for symmetry on the occasion of his first wedding, to Helena Friese), to complete plans for the memorial tablet.

Tea was taken in the Commercial Rooms with

Two generations of Friese-Greenes, Reece and the Lord Mayor at the unveiling, 1955.

the president, Bertram Davis, acting on behalf of the QEH Old Boys, followed by group portraits before the unveiling at 12 College Street at 6.00 pm. There they waited five minutes for thc BBC recording cars to signal that the mike was warmed up! Reece introduced the Lord Mayor, Alderman Harry Crook (of Kleeneze fame), hoping the threat of demolition would be lifted and asking him to unveil the plaque set up on behalf of the seven organisations whom Reece had persuaded to play a part: the Savages, the Civic Society, the Western Counties Photographic Federation, lnstitute of British Photographers, Bristol Amateur Cine Sociey, Bristol Photographic Society and his own Bristol Camera Club, as well as Bristolians. Crook replied referring to the revolution of social habits of millions caused by the invention of cinematography. Reece ended 'Friese-Greene day' with a public lecture on Friese-Greene's life with lantern slides, claiming that he was more than simply a pioneer.

The follow up was a campaign to reprieve No 12, if necessary islanding it each side of new roads, to avoid the Corporation' s favourite ploy for demolition of historic buildings. (The site in fact turned out to be a temporary car park that may still be seen today.) Would Bristol Corporation desist if the cinematography industry would support a museum here with benevolent accommodation for retired members? When the Ministry of Works upgraded the Georgian house to Grade II from Grade III it seemed that Reece had won. But no offers were forthcoming from the industry and with a remarkable sleight of hand the Corporation ignored the listing and demolished, starting on January 25th and finishing on February 17th 1958. Reece managed to save the bottom step! There was then the issue of the future of the plaque. Reece did not fail to grasp that the new Lord Mayor, Alderman Chamberlain, was himself a proprietor of Bristol cinemas and after much debate and with Chamberlain's support it was agreed that the plaque be reset on the rear of the Council House, facing the site of No 12.

Friese-Greene day produced an almost immediate counter to Reece's claims in the form of an article from a photo-historian from Eastman Kodak. In retrospect, the very speed and orchestration may yet prove the undoing of the detractors' case. Tony Friese-Greene and Reece were quick to realise when given the chance to do a joint BBC broadcast in America in the autumn of 1955.' ...We should leave a mark that will sow doubts in the most ardent Edison admirers in America.' When dealing with an inventor with more than seventy patents to his name, at least five prefiguring major technological developments of the twentieth century (1890 printing postcards, 1895 photo-typesetting, 1896 X-rays, 1897 inkless printing, 1905 *Bio-colour* movie film), the contemporary decision on movie camera patent in his favour by the American courts and the views of his associate and the industry at the time of his death, one would have to marshal considerable new evidence to disprove so strong a claim. Fortunately it seems in this the opponents of Friese-Greene failed.

They preferred first to rely only on contemporary published reports - by no means conclusive as anyone familiar with dealing with published papers is aware. Then Monsieur Le Prince was optioned as the best candidate for inventor - a man who was known to have disappeared together with his equipment whilst travelling in France before validation was made and who was never found! It was quite overlooked that the claims of three others who each made preliminary or subsequent discoveries had Friese-Greene as their partner in common. It was then claimed that the patent camera did not work, could not work and anyway the necessary projector was absent. Faced with a carefully engineered patent drawing it is not enough to simply claim it would not work without giving reasons - it must be demonstrated that the principles would not work. As for the projector, a red herring too. How could it be justifiably maintained that the camera was not the progenitor of moving pictures? Finally they ignored the significance of the principles of the movie camera - the flexible film strip moving forward behind a trailing loop (the importance of this is stressed by Winton Johnson in an unpublished manuscript) - central to the Friese-Greene patent. All this came from a side with a vested interest in the reputation of Edison who held a patent of later date in the U.S. only and who, in his lifetime, did not seek to claim the invention for himself.

Doubtless there is much still to be decided as to the true extent of Friese-Greene's achievements, but that will only come (in so far as is now possible with the distance of time) with proper detachment.

The shape of things to come:
the new Hollywood-style multiplex which opened in Bristol in the summer of 1994
(photo: courtesy of the Bristol Evening Post)

The End